IN SEARCH OF ERNEST HEMINGWAY

IN SEARCH
OF ERNEST HEMINGWAY

A MODEL FOR TEACHING
A LITERATURE SEMINAR

BROOKE WORKMAN
West High School, Iowa City

National Council of Teachers of English
1111 Kenyon Road, Urbana, Illinois 61801

Grateful acknowledgment is made for permission to reprint the following material. "A Telephone Call to Mary Hemingway" by Brooke Workman, which first appeared in *Today's Education*, September-October 1976. Reprinted by permission of the National Education Association. "Air Line" by Ernest Hemingway. Copyright © 1979 by the Ernest Hemingway Foundation. Reprinted by permission of the Ernest Hemingway Foundation. "On the Blue Water: A Gulf Stream Letter" by Ernest Hemingway. Copyright 1936 by Esquire, Inc.; renewed © 1964 by Mary Hemingway. Reprinted by permission.

Book Design: Tom Kovacs

NCTE Stock Number 22892

Library of Congress Cataloging in Publication Data

Workman, Brooke, 1933–
    In search of Ernest Hemingway.

    Bibliography: p.
    1. Hemingway, Ernest, 1899-1961—Study and teaching (Secondary)—Outlines, syllabi, etc.   2. American literature—Study and teaching (Secondary)   I. Title.
    PS3515.E37Z954   813'.5'2   79-452
    ISBN 0-8141-2289-2

To Leslie and Mark !

CONTENTS

List of Handouts   ix

Preface   xi

Acknowledgments   xv

Introduction   xvii

Orientation to the Seminar   1
     Days 1–2

Paper I: "Indian Camp"   11
     Days 3–10

Paper II: *The Sun Also Rises*   19
     Days 11–26

Paper III: *A Farewell to Arms*   31
     Days 27–42

Paper IV: A Profile of Ernest Hemingway   41
     Days 43–57

Paper V: Paper of Choice   57
     Days 58–69

Paper VI: *The Old Man and the Sea*   67
     Days 70–79

Paper VII: The Summing Up   77
     Days 80–90

Appendix A   93

Appendix B   96

Appendix C   100

Appendix D   103

Bibliography   107

HANDOUTS

1. Tentative Schedule   3
2. The Hemingway Chronology   7
3. The Position Paper   9
4. Suggestions for Paper I: "Indian Camp"   14
5. Student Model for Paper I   15
6. Suggestions for Paper II: *The Sun Also Rises*   23
7. Student Model for Paper II   24
8. Suggestions for Paper III: *A Farewell to Arms*   35
9. Student Model for Paper III   36
10. Suggestions for Paper IV: The Profile Paper   45
11. Student Model for Paper IV: Use of Biography   46
12. Student Model for Paper IV: Combining Biography
    and Literature   52
13. Suggestions for Paper V: Paper of Choice   60
14. Student Model for Paper V   62
15. Suggestions for Paper VI: *The Old Man and the Sea*   71
16. Student Model for Paper VI   72
17. Suggestions for Paper VII: Summing Up   79
18. Suggestions for Paper VII: Parody   80
19. Student Model for Paper VII: Summing Up   81
20. Student Model for Paper VII: Parody   86
21. Seminar Evaluation   89

PREFACE

WHY NOT A SEMINAR?

I have taught American literature courses in high school for more than eighteen years, but the broad survey outlines which served me in the 1950s—Puritans to the Present—began to narrow in the late 1960s. The title remained, but I began to pursue the change of form and content in American literature that took place after Theodore Dreiser's *Sister Carrie* (1900). I would use nineteenth-century writers like Poe, Thoreau, Dickinson, Melville, and Whitman to suggest the changes that were to emerge after World War I.

My shift from broad survey to more narrowed focus gained momentum as West High School of Iowa City became caught up in the curriculum revolution of the 60s, a revolution that called for shorter courses, even mini-courses. Relevance, we called it. Slices of American literature became courses: Ethnic American Novels, The American Short Story. Sometimes courses combined three or four authors, reminiscent of graduate school "bedfellow courses"—Twain, Faulkner, Salinger. Strange bedfellows at times.

As year courses became semester and finally trimester courses, I reflected on the problems created by fragmenting literature, and I recalled a tactic I had used in 1962 while teaching for the Overseas Schools run by the U.S. government in West Germany. In an American literature survey course for high-ability juniors and seniors, I had assigned a position paper on one American author. The paper required a single focus based on the reading of at least five of the author's works and one hundred pages of biography and/or autobiography. I had personally followed a similar in-depth reading practice for years, and I hoped to share with students what I had discovered through understanding a writer's basic themes and style—a sense of how biography relates to literary material, the joy of expertise which includes a knowledge of major and minor works and their chronology, a delight in quotable lines, and the privilege of choosing favorite characters. In sum, this process can make a writer come alive, become a friend (or enemy). And the assignment worked. Many of those former students have, in fact, told me that their first genuine response to literature came as a result of the in-depth study of James, Cather, Steinbeck, Hemingway. They also observed that the position paper had been a valuable college preparatory experience.

So I introduced the scheme at Iowa City West. Or, rather, I decided to transform an individual term paper course into a seminar that would follow the American literature survey course. The seminar, that in-depth approach that entered American universities back in the 1860s, seemed an appropriate structure since it combines individual study with small group interaction. Instead of a single synthesis paper, however, my fifteen juniors and seniors wrote seven position papers. Instead of grading all of the papers for each assignment, I graded all but two; these two were evaluated by the group. Naturally the assignments were chronological, though there was an author profile paper near the middle of the term and a summation paper at the end. Classroom activities included not only reading and writing and evaluation (we called the group evaluation of papers "Defense Day"), but also the oral reading of short works, the use of audio-visual materials, brief teacher "lectures," and bulletin board displays. Eventually we even contacted authors (see Appendix A) and had weekend parties for which we dressed as literary characters.

The idea flourished. Beginning with an experimental seminar four years ago on F. Scott Fitzgerald, I have gone on to offer seminars on John Steinbeck, William Saroyan, J.D. Salinger, and Ernest Hemingway—all authors chosen by students. In fact, students have elected three times to devote the seminar to Hemingway. We have gone from one section to two and now three. The word seems to be out at West High that the seminar is fun, challenging, and a valuable skills course, especially in writing.

Certainly one of my initial fears was dispelled, the fear that I would be accused of teaching a very *specialized* course. The seminar's popularity with students and its acceptance by parents seem to indicate that a single-author seminar accenting basic writing skills and in-depth appreciation is a valuable contribution to the high school English program. Why not a seminar!

WHY HEMINGWAY?

Why Hemingway? Well, probably not for his poetry:

Air Line

! : , , .
, , ,
, : , !
—E.H.

As you will probably notice the above poem is blank verse.

But this 1916 poem,* written when Hemingway was seventeen years old, does say something about him and the brave new world of the early twentieth century. Kids like it, too, for it suggests that famous authors had fun in high school, had beginnings.

Studying Ernest Hemingway can be especially rewarding to high school students for at least five good reasons.

(1) Hemingway is famous, more so than almost any other author in American literature. He won the Nobel and Pulitzer Prizes, his works have been filmed, their titles remain current and familiar *(The Old Man and the Sea, A Farewell to Arms, For Whom the Bell Tolls)*. Hemingway has not gone out of style. There seems to be worth in studying somebody famous; the study may tell us something about fame and the staying power of writers.

*From Matthew Bruccoli, ed., *Ernest Hemingway's Apprenticeship: Oak Park, 1916-1917* (Washington, D.C.: Microcard Editions, 1971), p. 26.

(2) Hemingway was an interesting human being, a man of poetry and passion, of various interests that appeal to many teenagers—fishing, hunting, bullfighting, boxing. He liked to be on the road to exotic places—Paris, Spain, Cuba, Africa. And he played many roles in his lifetime: rebellious teenager, soldier, disenchanted lover, expatriate, reporter and war correspondent, husband (four times), son and father, male chauvinist, public and private man, writer of wealth and success.

(3) Learning about Hemingway's world and reading his books reveal much about America during the first half of the twentieth century. Students begin to understand how the quiet, rural life changed after World War I, how many people left their Oak Parks for the East Coast, even for Europe. To study Hemingway is to learn about the American family, about World Wars I and II and the Spanish Civil War, about writers like Sherwood Anderson, Ezra Pound, James Joyce, Gertrude Stein, F. Scott Fitzgerald, William Faulkner, about American and world geography (Illinois, Michigan, Paris, Pamplona, Milan, Key West, Cuba, Idaho), about famous people from Marlene Dietrich to Fidel Castro.

(4) Hemingway's work can be read on many levels. First, the prose is concrete, direct, simple in construction but often poetic; it was built on practical newspaper experience, on theory after Hemingway studied Stein, Anderson, Joyce, and others, and on hard work. Hemingway is a model of writing discipline, and students are drawn to his style, sometimes imitating it unconsciously and sometimes parodying it. Second, the plots and characters are both simple and complex. They invite re-reading. Nick Adams, the innocent teenager, evolves into the wounded Jake Barnes, one of several life-explorers in Hemingway who search for "grace under pressure" in Italy, Africa, Cuba. Male and female—Frederic Henry and Santiago, Brett Ashley and Catherine Barkley—Hemingway's characters live by a code that students try to define. Finally, individual students relate to individual works, discovering meaning even in the so-called weak novels like *Across the River and into the Trees,* and they begin to understand why critics find certain works to be "major."

(5) Not all questions about Hemingway can be answered. At the end of the seminar, there is satisfaction, yet there is also an edge of dissatis-

faction. Not everything is laid to rest. Why did Hemingway write so much about death? Was his suicide a violation of his own Code? Was he religious? What would he think about the books published after his death, such as *Islands in the Stream?*

Ernest Hemingway makes an excellent beginning.

ACKNOWLEDGMENTS

I would like to thank all those Iowa City West High School students whose enthusiasm and hard work made successful seminars over the past four years possible, especially those juniors and seniors who contributed position papers to this handbook: Mark Champe, Pat Chong, Melody Myers, Dan Goldberg, Amy Freeman, Emily Buss, Anne Nusser, Greg Pope, and Louise Milkman.

INTRODUCTION: THE SEMINAR METHOD

This handbook is designed to be used every day for a semester and includes a schedule, lesson plans, material for reproduction and distribution, and a serviceable Hemingway bibliography. It is based not only on a theory about how students improve basic writing skills and acquire new reading habits, but also on four years of experience with high school students at West High School in Iowa City, Iowa. Through trial and error, from student suggestions and papers, with the discovery of new materials, the handbook evolved.

This handbook, then, is the result of my own search, not so much for Ernest Hemingway or any other author, but for a vital teaching method. I wanted my students to enjoy literature and to develop their critical reading skills in a way that no survey course would allow. From personal experience I knew that the in-depth exploration of a single author could provide an opening wedge to all of literature. Microcosm, macrocosm, if you will. So I designed a course in which in-depth analysis was shared by a group of students. Eventually this course design led to a major discovery: I had found a vital method not only for the teaching of *literature* but also for the teaching of *writing*.

THE OVERALL DESIGN OF THE COURSE

A good handbook, however pragmatic, must be flexible if it is to meet the requirements of different schools, students, teachers. This particular handbook grew out of a trimester elective for fifteen students, some very gifted in reading and writing, some merely interested in literature and self-improvement. The only prerequisite for the seminar was an American literature survey course. Students in the first seminars chose an author from all of American literature; later

ones often asked to repeat an author who they had heard was exciting to study: Ernest Hemingway. Each seminar met for fifty days, and each student wrote seven position papers. Five of these were graded by the instructor and two were graded by the group. Final grades were based on the seven papers, on contributions to discussion and evaluation, and on growth. Classroom dynamics varied; the fifty-five minutes could be charged with volatile interaction or marked by quiet, thoughtful study. Always the spirit was cooperative. The seminar was great fun to teach.

Admittedly, the fifty class days were busy, so much so that the schedule included here has been revised to cover ninety class periods or an eighteen-week semester. This expanded format allows time to explore areas that could not be fully covered during a trimester—follow-up discussions, reference to critical opinion, in-class reading and writing time. Then, too, the schedule needs flexibility to allow for normal interruptions—assemblies, special events, snow days. Some instructors may want to include resource persons, telephone interviews (see Appendix A), an eighth paper, conferences with individual students, and formal testing. Finally, seminars are not just for the gifted, though the gifted enjoy the structure and content of such a course. More time is required to improve the skills of slower readers, less competent writers.

Having taught for twenty years, I am well aware of two hazards in teaching any course: work load and boredom. Let me begin by saying that this course is not a case study of Ernest Hemingway meant to be taught by a Hemingway expert or even a teacher who has taken a graduate seminar on Hemingway. The reading assignments pose no real burden since time is built into the schedule for much of the reading of the required short story and three novels. Since the instructor is not expected to be an expert, he or she joins the seminar in much of the discovery process. As for reading and correcting student papers, time is also built into the schedule for that, plus the bonus of Defense Day evaluations of two papers by the entire seminar. And while I believe that teachers should stress to administrators that the seminar is a writing course, one that works best with fifteen students, I have tried to open up the semester schedule to make the design feasible for larger classes. Thus, I do not see the instructional load of this course to be any more burdensome than, for example, an American literature survey course.

I have found little boredom in a course that explores an attractive writer through a variety of experiences. Following the logic of chronology, so important in suggesting the development of major themes, I first selected a short story ("Indian Camp") that would define the Hemingway material. Its brevity allowed time for the in-class oral reading of additional stories, for a discussion of what makes a position paper, and for an introduction to Defense Day. Perhaps even more significantly, there was time to develop rapport within the seminar. The next two assignments dealt with longer works, *The Sun Also Rises* and *A Farewell to Arms,* two novels which invited comparison with each other and with the earlier stories. By the fourth paper, students had begun to see the autobiographical nature of the writing and were ready to deal with Hemingway the man and writer. This assignment required individual research which allowed students to take even more personal positions than they had been able to take based on in-common readings. The fifth assignment, based on a reading of choice, also encouraged individuality by offering students the opportunity to present works that others may not have read. *The Old Man and the Sea,* the sixth assignment, again brought the class together in a common and important final reading. The seventh paper had its own special delights: no reading but a good deal of reflection (if students chose summation) or creativity (if students tried imitation or parody). This sequence of seven writing assignments, reinforced by resource materials such as films, provided an antidote to boredom for students and teacher alike.

While the content has its appeal, the real vitality of the seminar design came from the position papers and the Defense Days. In fact, it was here I discovered that I was teaching a vital writing course. It soon became obvious that students were not only learning about the writing of Ernest Hemingway, but also about their own writing. The interaction of the seven written assignments made its impact, though no student ever referred to the seminar as a "writing course."

Each of the three-to-five-page, typed assignments was defined as a "position paper" because students were asked to limit their analysis to a single focus. This position was to be organized, supported by concrete detail, and mechanically sound. Since the readings were chronological, students were encouraged to build their papers upon each other, to use comparison and contrast. Writing goals were sequential, ranging from concern with proofreading and clarity to the more complex skills of documentation and synthesis. A model student paper for each of the seven assignments is included in the text.

Defense Day offered a dramatic focus for each assignment. While the instructor provided an audience for all of the position papers, two papers were read and evaluated by the entire seminar. In addition, there was an element of surprise since students did not know which papers would be chosen for a given Defense Day until all had been handed in and copies of the papers to be analyzed were made. When Defense Day arrived, two students shared their papers with the class. With the instructor acting as a classroom manager, not evaluator, members of the seminar used three criteria to respond to each paper: (1) clarity of position, (2) organization and support, and (3) mechanics. Together students arrived at a consensus grade for each paper.

Obviously, Defense Day is a time of tension. For the student facing a peer audience, there are the questions that all writers must face: Will they understand my position? Is my position supported by concrete detail? Is it mechanically sound—at least sound enough to satisfy my readers? Will I be able to respond to their questions and criticisms? What will be the final assessment? Since each student appears on two Defense Days, there is the natural concern that the second be as good as, if not better than, the first.

But Defense Day has its rewards. Since everyone comes up for Defense Day, everyone both evaluates and is evaluated. Thus, the spirit of Defense Day becomes one of cooperation. Students work together to help each other become better writers; they learn from each other as well as from the instructor. With each Defense Day, students acquire more experience in discussing and implementing the criteria of good writing. The evaluation of the Defense Day papers and of their own papers, which are returned by the instructor at the end of the day, prepares student writers for future writing assignments. Indeed, one of the major goals of the writing design becomes obvious: The Next Paper. And finally, each student has a better understanding of his or her own writing. The search for Ernest Hemingway inevitably leads home.

But this handbook is only a beginning. While it details assignments and suggests a number of concrete ways to exploit Hemingway material, its essential design can be applied to the study of other authors. I have explored four other authors in similar seminars. I chose each because I thought that author would be fun, not because I was an expert on that literary figure. And it was fun to teach F. Scott Fitzgerald (though one should never begin with *This Side of Paradise*), John Steinbeck (though *The Grapes of Wrath* is long), William Saroyan (though some of my students thought Bill must not be too bright with his always cosmic optimism), and J. D. Salinger (though he has resisted biographers and interviewers). Since teachers know their own interests and audiences, I will not go beyond suggesting these four writers. I do know that I would have great difficulty taking high school students through the likes of William Faulkner and Henry James. I do know that I am presently considering Richard Wright and Mark Twain. I also think that the design would work well with short story writers, science fiction writers, playwrights, and even poets.

WRITING ASSIGNMENTS

While the papers and discussions build upon themselves, the instructor may wish to emphasize a sequence of writing skills. For example,

when writing assignments are made or during Defense Day, the instructor may want to announce concrete goals for writing improvement. The following developmental sequence for the seven position papers has been useful:

Paper I: "Indian Camp"

1. Following format directions is important for the initial paper: 3–5 pages, typed manuscript form.

2. The idea of a single clear position is essential for the first paper.

Paper II: *The Sun Also Rises*

1. Emphasize the use of concrete examples from the book. Ask students to use at least one direct quotation from the novel to document the position and to give "flavor" to the material.

2. Stress introductions and conclusions. What the reader reads first and last is essential in the psychology of writing.

3. Reiterate the need for careful proofreading.

Paper III: *A Farewell to Arms*

1. Stress transitions between sentences and paragraphs. Does the paper flow logically? Do connectives help to unify it? Does the organization serve to clarify the single position? Does the introduction suggest the body of the paper? Does the position find its final definition in the conclusion?

2. Encourage students to work on sentence variety. Are the sentences appealing—not all simple or compound sentences, not all beginning with the subject-verb pattern ("Catherine felt," "She said . . . ")

3. Urge students to purchase a paperback copy of *Roget's Thesaurus*. Instruct them on its use with a class copy.

Paper IV: Profile of Ernest Hemingway

1. Encourage students to use both biographical and literary material in formulating a position.

2. Discuss the need for footnotes and bibliography and provide a style sheet of correct forms. You may also wish to

discuss how to edit a direct quotation, how to build a smooth transition from the text to the direct quotation, when to single space direct quotations and when to incorporate them into the double-spaced text.

3. It might be interesting to discuss teacher and student "pet peeves" regarding style. For example, some people detest "a lot" in papers, while others believe that the first-person "I" has no place in formal writing.

Paper V: Student Choice

1. A clear plot summary and precise character descriptions are essential for a successful choice paper because many Defense Day evaluators will not have read the work under consideration.

2. Encourage students to relate previous in-common readings to the work of their choice. Comparison and contrast are useful techniques, especially for college-bound students.

3. An amusing aside: ask students if they are beginning to write like Ernest Hemingway. Unconscious imitation is one of the "hazards" of studying an author in depth.

Paper VI: *The Old Man and the Sea*

1. Since tone is so important in this novel, you may wish to discuss how style affects the mood of student papers. If a student has a serious theme about the poetic nature of a work, like this one, he or she may use serious and poetic techniques, such as similes, metaphors, symbols.

2. Since Hemingway was absorbed by matters of style, you might suggest special writing techniques, e.g., (1) repetition, such as nearly repeating a line or using the same beginning for two sentences in a row; (2) variation, such as using a tight, short sentence to follow a long one—to catch the eye, to summarize, to punctuate.

3. Insist on careful proofreading and a minimum number of mechanical errors.

Paper VII: Summing Up

1. Encourage students to use ideas from their previous papers and those of other students. This assignment is a lesson in synthesis.

2. If you intend to encourage humor or parody in the final assignment, a review of these approaches is in order.

3. Students should be reminded of the oral nature of the final assignment. All final papers are read aloud and will not be available for prior study as in previous Defense Day situations. Ask students, therefore, to read their papers aloud to themselves until they are satisfied, not only with their reading, but also with their writing—especially word choice and cadence.

DEFENSE DAY

Successful Defense Days depend on the clarity with which the assignment was given. Discussions of how to narrow an idea to a single position should prevent papers with a lack of focus. The student model of a *typed* three-to-five-page paper and the caution that papers will be reproduced throughout the seminar should ensure satisfactory form.

The primary goal of Defense Day is to reinforce in positive ways the defender, as well as the entire seminar. Defense Day is not Destruction Day. Evaluation and grading should be supportive for future writers and defenders. It is a day of sharing, learning, and allaying fears. It is therefore important that you select good models, especially for the first defense: papers with careful typing for acceptable reproduction, papers of the specified length with a clear position and good writing. You need not choose the two best papers (or four, if your class is large and you run two consecutive Defense Days), but your choices should generally be strong papers. Conflicting viewpoints, if equally well written, can be very stimulating for the first discussion.

After you have selected the Defense Day papers, make copies for each student in the class. The copies (with or without the student's name) should be distributed during the class period before Defense Day (see Handout 1: Tentative

Schedule) so that students have time to read and annotate them. Advance distribution also generates interest since students often discuss the papers among themselves before Defense Day. Keep the original papers; you will note the results of the Defense Day evaluation on each one before returning it to the author.

Defense Day begins with calm and some humor. Remind the class that it is difficult to go first, to set an example; it is also difficult to evaluate each other. Remind the present defenders that they have the delight of finishing first and subsequent opportunities to evaluate papers. Remind the class that everyone is trying to learn from each other, to improve, to enjoy studying the author chosen by the seminar. (Note: students should bring not only the defense papers to class, but also the works under discussion for possible reference.)

Two papers work well in a normal class period of approximately fifty minutes. Asking each defender to read his or her paper aloud gives everyone a chance to re-read the paper, to hear how the author emphasizes the ideas, and to make final notations. After the oral reading, the discussion should focus on three evaluative criteria: clarity of position, adequacy of supporting evidence and logical development, and mechanics. Discussing and grading a paper takes a full twenty-five minutes.

Criterion one: clarity of position. After the defender has read the paper, ask a seminar member to state the position of that paper. Summarize what the student has said to confirm that you and the class understand his or her understanding of the paper's position. Now call on another seminar member to see if he or she agrees with the interpretation of the first student. If disagreement arises, however slight, call on other members until a consensus position emerges. Of course, some students may feel that no consensus is possible or that the position of the paper is unclear.

Finally, return to the defender and ask if he or she agrees with the interpretation of a given student or with the class consensus. The defender should be allowed to reflect on his or her position and to clarify that position to those who found it unclear.

Criterion two: organization and support. After the definition of the position, consider how the author organized and supported that position. The instructor, the defender, and the seminar should review the basic outline of the paper (Introduction, Body, Conclusion); the procedure for developing a single focus; and the concrete use of plot, characters, and quotations to support generalizations. Basic questions can be asked: Is the position clear because it is logical? Is it clear because it is supported by direct reference and quotation? Does the paper stay on target or is it sidetracked by irrelevancies or the overemphasis of a minor point? Does the introduction suggest the position? Does the conclusion restate it? Is the title well chosen?

After the organization and supporting detail have been clarified, seminar members should be encouraged to react again to the position. Even if they disagree with the position, they should ask themselves whether or not it is well defended. If the position is well defended, why do some members of the seminar continue to disagree with it? This discussion is often lively, and students should be reminded that during the next class period there will be time to pursue these positions, as well as to learn what critics have said about them.

Criterion three: mechanics. Finally, seminar members should react to the paper's mechanics, page by page. Do errors distract the reader from the paper's content? Do the mechanical problems stem from poor proofreading or are they obvious errors in spelling, capitalization, usage, paragraphing? What about style—awkward sentences, imprecise or inadequate word choices, inappropriate tone, insensitivity to nuance? While this critical examination should not become an exercise in nitpicking, seminar members and especially the instructor should make clear that the clarity of a paper's position is heavily dependent on the writer's skill with mechanics.

While some instructors prefer to evaluate student papers themselves, the papers chosen for Defense Day should be graded by the group. Defense Day has its own surprises, delights, and tensions, but it should also have a cooperative spirit. One successful technique is to return to the student who originally tried to state the paper's position. That student first posed the immediate problem of clarity. Ask that student to suggest a grade and to justify it. Then move to other students, asking for grades and justifications, reminding them that the discussion has emphasized clarity of position, over-all organization, adequacy of supporting evidence, and mechanics. Almost always, a consensus emerges, though the seminar may want the instructor to add his or her grade. If possible, avoid adding your grade because it tends to weigh too heavily and may make students suspicious that their opinions are secondary.

Obviously, peer grading creates tensions. Classroom friends (and enemies) find it difficult to be objective. You may feel that consensus grades are sometimes too high. The grades given at Defense Day should not, however, be seen as a diminution of "standards," for the total learning experience of Defense Day is more important than any single grade. And, as a matter of fact, my experience with four years of Defense Days indicates that students are not only generally fair but usually assign grades that are very close to my private evaluation. The seminar should never lose *its* focus: the next paper, the student wanting to write that paper and to make it even better than the last paper.

After the completion of two defense papers (or four if Defense Day is extended to two days), return graded papers to all students. They will need them for open discussion at the next class period. In addition, return the original papers of the defenders with your comments, a summary of the comments made by the seminar during the discussion, and the consensus grade.

ADAPTING THE SEMINAR TO OTHER AUTHORS

The Hemingway seminar concretizes a *process* of reading, discussion, writing, and evaluation that can be transferred to other authors, other seminars. The process, established with the first paper and repeated and reinforced throughout the semester, follows these steps:

1. Orientation: providing literary, historical, and biographical background to students
2. Reading source materials orally and individually, class discussion, audio-visual materials, and mini-lectures
3. Choosing a paper topic: teacher suggestions and papers written by students from previous seminars

4. Writing, revising, and proofreading the paper
5. Evaluation: Defense Day and Follow-up

Although the process remains relatively constant, the content of the seminar itself may change. While Ernest Hemingway is an excellent choice, the seminar can be built around other literary figures. Selecting an author and the specific works to be considered is, of course, important since students must "live" with that author for eighteen weeks.

How, then, should the author be determined?

First, there are practical considerations. Ideally you might wish to have students use the first days of the course to select an author, but this tactic will create practical problems of time (and budget!) for ordering or otherwise securing books. Some instructors are willing to assemble materials through libraries, used book stores, and student copies, but many teachers want the security of books ordered in advance. Even when the practical problems of student selection can be overcome, the method has its hazards. Students usually have not read most of the materials and may be disappointed in or thwarted by their own choice. For example, they may blithely disregard your warning that authors like William Faulkner, Henry James, or even Saul Bellow pose problems—length, level of difficulty—for many high school students.

Second, you may have a favorite author and feel inclined to settle on that writer for the seminar. Such motivation is not necessarily sinister, for your own background and preferences can go a long way in creating a successful seminar. Certainly you may find teenage students less than enchanted with your choice of author, but this method of selection is a good risk, especially if you keep teenage interests in mind. And it does solve the practical problem of advance book orders.

Third, you may wish to rely on the experience of others—other teachers in the school or the following list of authors and titles previously taught at West High School. All were successful seminars, although Steinbeck and Salinger were probably more appealing to teenagers than Fitzgerald and Saroyan.

I have included below the seven writing assignments for each of the four authors I have used in alternate versions of the Hemingway seminar.

F. Scott Fitzgerald

Paper I: "The Rich Boy" (1926)

Paper II: *This Side of Paradise* (1920)

Paper III: *The Great Gatsby* (1925)

Paper IV: Profile

Paper V: "Babylon Revisited" (1930)

Paper VI: Student Choice

Paper VII: Summation

John Steinbeck

Paper I: "The Harness" (1938)

Paper II: *Tortilla Flat* (1935)

Paper III: *Of Mice and Men* (1937)

Paper IV: *The Grapes of Wrath* (1939)

Paper V: Profile

Paper VI: Student Choice

Paper VII: Summation

William Saroyan

Paper I: "The Daring Young Man on the Flying Trapeze" (1934)

Paper II: *The Time of Your Life* (1939)

Paper III: "The Pomegranate Trees" (1940)

Paper IV: *The Human Comedy* (1943)

Paper V: Profile

Paper VI: Student Choice

Paper VII: Summation

J. D. Salinger

Paper I: "A Perfect Day for Bananafish" (1948)

Paper II: *The Catcher in the Rye* (1951)

Paper III: "Teddy" (1953)

Paper IV: *Franny and Zooey* (1961)

Paper V: Profile

Paper VI: Student Choice

Paper VII: Summation

However you select an author, you will be wise to maintain the chronological presentation, to offer student choices, to require papers on both short and long works, and to schedule a profile paper near the middle of the course when students are becoming increasingly interested in the writer and the autobiographical nature of his or her works.

But enough. You have the Map of the Territory. It works. And you and your students should make good company in your search for Ernest Hemingway and other American writers. The trip will be memorable, more than snapshots and color slides. How I envy you in your first exploration!

ORIENTATION TO THE SEMINAR
DAYS 1-2

DAY 1: GETTING ACQUAINTED WITH THE COURSE AND EACH OTHER

Goals

1. To acquaint students with the nature of the seminar and to introduce them to its method and content.
2. To help students get to know each other.

Materials

1. Handout 1: Tentative Schedule.
2. After you have taught the seminar, use evaluations from former students (see Day 90) to interest beginning students.

Procedure

1. Using Handout 1 as a guide, offer an overview of the course, noting particularly how writing and reading activities are correlated. Point out the variety in the course, the value of studying an author in depth, the fact that the course offers an opportunity to improve writing skills as well as opportunities for individual exploration and group discussion.
2. Stress that you genuinely want to know the students and to have them know each other. Everyone will be working together in the course.
3. Pair off students who do not know each other or who know each other only slightly. Find a partner for yourself. Ask each student to interview his or her partner without taking notes, asking questions that each partner would like answered—family, job, favorite food, sports, music, travel, plans for the future.
4. After five or ten minutes, ask each student to introduce his or her partner to the seminar by summarizing the answers to the interview questions. Now the class has taken its first step toward becoming a genuine seminar. These introductions may lead to friendships, and they will certainly help to establish the understanding and cooperation needed in later discussions, especially the evaluations on Defense Day.

Additional Suggestion

A classroom bulletin board on Ernest Hemingway helps to develop interest: photographs, magazine clippings, a sample position paper (one from this handbook or from a previous seminar), maps (Illinois, Michigan, Florida, Idaho, France, Italy, Cuba, Spain). Perhaps some students have visited the geographical settings of Hemingway's life and literature and have materials to contribute to an evolving bulletin board.

DAY 2: INTRODUCING HEMINGWAY AND THE POSITION PAPER

Goals

1. To preview Hemingway's life and work.
2. To introduce the Position Paper.

Materials

1. Handout 2: The Hemingway Chronology. You may also refer to the materials on Hemingway's life and times and his family in Appendix B.
2. Handout 3: The Position Paper.

Procedure

1. Referring to Handout 2: The Hemingway Chronology, discuss the idea that the seminar will be one of discovery, of learning how Hemingway's ideas and writing developed.

The first of the seven position papers focuses on the Nick Adams stories of the 1920s. In particular, the paper will formulate a position about "Indian Camp," an early short story that was written in Paris after World War I and appeared in a small book, *In Our Time.*

2. Note that Hemingway's life carried him from his boyhood home in Oak Park, a suburb of Chicago, to a summer home near Petoskey in upper Michigan, the setting for "Indian Camp." The family enjoyed the change of scenery and fishing (a life-long enthusiasm of the author), and Dr. Hemingway carried on his medical practice there by treating the local Ojibway Indians. Go on to observe that Hemingway moved out into the world after he graduated from high school: a cub reporter in Kansas City, World War I service in Italy, newspaper work in Toronto, expatriate life in Paris in the 1920s, trips throughout his life to Spain, Key West, Africa, Cuba, and Ketchum, Idaho.

3. Distribute Handout 3: The Position Paper and discuss the nature of a position paper. Stress the requirements of length and format (typed, double-spaced, one side, unlined paper) since clear, complete copies must be distributed for Defense Day. At this point, do not dwell on evaluation procedures since a positive attitude toward writing does not begin with apprehension about grades. Remind students that typing is required by most college teachers and that it is wise to improve their typing now. Tell them that you will provide position papers written by high school juniors and seniors for them to examine; assure them that they will be given considerable class time for reading and writing. Useful background material and even suggestions for topics will be given as specific papers are assigned.

Additional Suggestion

Some students may already have read books by or about Hemingway. Encourage them to share their initial impressions.

HANDOUT 1
TENTATIVE SCHEDULE FOR SEMINAR IN AMERICAN LITERATURE:
ERNEST HEMINGWAY

Orientation to the Seminar

Day 1.   Getting acquainted with the course and each other
Day 2.   Introducing Hemingway and the Position Paper

Paper I: "Indian Camp" (1925)

Day 3.   Reading aloud and discussion of "Up in Michigan" (1923) and "The Doctor and the Doctor's Wife" (1925)
ASSIGNMENT: Position Paper on "Indian Camp"
Due: _____
Day 4.   Reading aloud and discussion of "The End of Something" (1925)
Day 5.   Reading aloud and discussion of "Three Day Blow" (1925)
Day 6.   Suggestions for Position Paper on "Indian Camp" and in-class writing
Day 7.   Reading aloud and discussion of "Ten Indians" (1927)
Day 8.   In-class writing
Day 9.   Reading aloud and discussion of "The Battler" (1925)
Position Paper on "Indian Camp" due
Day 10. Film: *My Old Man* (story published 1923)

Paper II: "The Sun Also Rises" (1926)

Day 11. Introduction to *The Sun Also Rises;* begin reading
ASSIGNMENT: Position Paper on *The Sun Also Rises*
Due: _____
Day 12. Reading
Day 13. Discussion: Life in Paris in the 1920s
Day 14. Reading
Day 15. Reading
Day 16. Reading and/or distribution of Defense Day papers
Day 17. Defense Day: "Indian Camp"
Day 18. Follow-up discussion: students and critics
Day 19. Film: *Hemingway's Spain: "The Sun Also Rises"*
Day 20. Reading
Day 21. Suggestions for Position Paper on *The Sun Also Rises* and reading or writing
Day 22. Film: *Hemingway's Spain: "Death in the Afternoon"*
Day 23. Reading aloud and discussion of "The Big Two-Hearted River" (1925)
Day 24. Reading aloud and discussion of "The Big Two-Hearted River"
Day 25. In-class writing and proofreading
Day 26. Reading aloud and discussion of "In Another Country" (1927)
Position Paper on *The Sun Also Rises* due

Paper III: "A Farewell to Arms" (1929)

Day 27.   Introduction to *A Farewell to Arms;* begin reading
ASSIGNMENT: Position Paper on *A Farewell to Arms*
Due: _____

Day 28.   Reading

Day 29.   Reading

Day 30.   Reading aloud and discussion of "Now I Lay Me" (1927) and "A Very Short Story" (1927)

Day 31.   Suggestions for Position Paper on *A Farewell to Arms* and in-class reading

Day 32.   Discussion: World War I and Hemingway, Dr. Hemingway's suicide, Key West

Day 33.   Reading; distribution of papers for Defense Day

Day 34.   Defense Day: *The Sun Also Rises*

Day 35.   Follow-up discussion: students and critics

Day 36.   Reading

Day 37.   Reading aloud and discussion of "Soldier's Home" (1925)

Day 38.   Reading

Day 39.   Reading and writing

Day 40.   Writing

Day 41.   Writing and proofreading

Day 42.   Reading aloud and discussion of "Fathers and Sons" (1933)
Position Paper on *A Farewell to Arms* due

Paper IV: A Profile of Ernest Hemingway

Day 43.   Review of the Hemingway biography and introduction to Profile Paper
ASSIGNMENT: Profile Paper developed from 100 pages of reading in Hemingway's biographers
Due: _____

Day 44.   Film: *Hemingway*

Day 45.   Reading and research for Anecdote Day

Day 46.   Reading and research for Anecdote Day

Day 47.   Anecdote Day

Day 48.   Anecdote Day

Day 49.   Reading; distribution of papers for Defense Day

Day 50.   Defense Day: *A Farewell to Arms*

Day 51.   Follow-up discussion: students and critics

Day 52.   Reading aloud and discussion of "A Clean Well-Lighted Place" (1933)

Day 53.   Reading

Day 54.   Reading, research, and writing

Day 55.   Writing

Day 56.   Writing and proofreading

Day 57. Reading aloud and discussion of "A Day's Wait" (1933) and "The Old Man at the Bridge" (1938)
Profile Paper on Ernest Hemingway due

Paper V: Your Choice

Day 58. Consideration of reading choices for Paper V
ASSIGNMENT: Position Paper on Hemingway work of student's choice
Due: _____

Day 59. Reading

Day 60. Reading

Day 61. Reading

Day 62. Reading; distribution of papers for Defense Day

Day 63. Defense Day: Profile Paper

Day 64. Defense Day: Profile Paper

Day 65. Follow-up discussion: students and critics

Day 66. Reading and writing

Day 67. Writing

Day 68. Writing and proofreading

Day 69. Reading aloud and discussion of "On the Blue Water" (1936)
Your Choice Paper due

Paper VI: "The Old Man and the Sea" (1952)

Day 70. Introduction to *The Old Man and the Sea;* begin reading
ASSIGNMENT: Position Paper on *The Old Man and the Sea*
Due: _____

Day 71. Reading

Day 72. Discussion: Hemingway and the Nobel Prize

Day 73. Suggestions for Position Paper on *The Old Man and the Sea*
and reading

Day 74. Reading, writing, and distribution of papers for Defense Day

Day 75. Defense Day: Your Choice Papers

Day 76. Follow-up discussion: students and critics

Day 77. Writing

Day 78. Writing and proofreading

Day 79. Previewing the Summation Paper
Position Paper on *The Old Man and the Sea* due

Paper VII: The Summing Up

Day 80. Reading, re-reading, research, and writing
ASSIGMENT: Summation Paper and/or a Humorous Paper on Hemingway and his work
Due: _____

Day 81.   Writing
Day 82.   Writing and distribution of papers for Defense Day
Day 83.   Defense Day: *The Old Man and the Sea*
Day 84.   Follow-up discussion: students and critics
Day 85.   Writing and proofreading
Day 86.   Reading aloud of final papers
Day 87.   Reading aloud of final papers
Day 88.   Reading aloud by instructor
Day 89.   Final discussion
Day 90.   Evaluation of seminar

HANDOUT 2
THE HEMINGWAY CHRONOLOGY

1899	Born in Oak Park, Illinois, the second of six children of Dr. Clarence Hemingway and Grace Hall Hemingway.
1917	Graduates from Oak Park High School. Rejected by U.S. Army because of eye injury from boxing. Works as cub reporter for the Kansas City *Star.*
1918	Goes to Italy as Red Cross ambulance driver. Legs severely injured by mortar fragments and heavy machine gun fire near Fossalta di Piave at midnight, July 8, 1918, two weeks before his nineteenth birthday.
1920–1924	Reporter and foreign correspondent for the Toronto *Star* and *Star Weekly.*
1921	Marries Hadley Richardson. Leaves for Europe.
1923	*Three Stories and Ten Poems* published in Paris; volume includes "Up in Michigan," "Out of Season," and "My Old Man."
1924	*in our time,* with thirty-six pages of miniatures, published in Paris.
1925	*In Our Time,* U.S. edition, published by Boni & Liveright. Fourteen short stories, plus the miniatures of the Paris edition, which are used as interchapters.
1926	*The Torrents of Spring,* published by Charles Scribner's Sons, New York publisher of all his subsequent books. *The Sun Also Rises* is published in October.
1927	Divorces Hadley Richardson. Marries Pauline Pfeiffer. Publication of *Men Without Women,* fourteen short stories, ten of which had appeared in magazines.
1928–1938	Lives in Key West, Florida. Suicide of his father (1928).
1929	*A Farewell to Arms,* Hemingway's first commercial success: 80,000 copies sold in four months.
1932	*Death in the Afternoon,* a nonfiction book about bullfighting.
1933	*Winner Take Nothing,* fourteen short stories. Publishes first of thirty-one articles and stories to appear in *Esquire* during the next six years.
1935	*Green Hills of Africa,* a nonfiction book about hunting.
1936–1937	Writes, speaks, raises money for the Loyalists in the Spanish Civil War.
1937	Covers the Spanish Civil War for the North American Newspaper Alliance. *To Have and Have Not,* three interconnected stories, two of which had been published separately.
1938	*The Fifth Column and the First Forty-Nine Stories,* which contains a play, short stories from previous collections, and seven short stories previously published in magazines.
1940	*For Whom the Bell Tolls,* his best-selling novel. Divorced by Pauline Pfeiffer. Marries Martha Gellhorn.

1942	*Men at War,* a collection of war stories and accounts with an introduction by Hemingway.
1943–1945	Covers the European theater of war as a newspaper and magazine correspondent.
1944	Divorced by Martha Gellhorn. Marries Mary Welsh.
1945–1959	Lives in Cuba at the Finca.
1950	*Across the River and into the Trees,* a much criticized novel.
1951	Death of Grace Hemingway, his mother.
1952	*The Old Man and the Sea,* first published in *Life* magazine. Awarded Pulitzer Prize.
1954	Wins the Nobel Prize, cited for "forceful and style-making mastery of the art of modern narration."
1959	Buys hunting lodge near Ketchum, Idaho.
1961	Death on July 2 of self-inflicted gunshot wounds; buried near Ketchum.
1964	*A Moveable Feast,* Paris essays and reminiscences.
1970	*Islands in the Stream,* an unfinished sea novel begun in the fall of 1950.

HANDOUT 3
THE POSITION PAPER

1. The position paper is just that: you adopt a single position about what you have read, a narrowed focus that can be developed by using concrete examples from the reading or from supplements to the reading. The position is *your* position.

2. The position paper must be three to five typed pages. The papers must be typed because at least two papers will be chosen from each assignment, reproduced, and evaluated during Defense Day by members of the seminar.

3. The possibilities for positions are nearly unlimited. You may want to develop an important quotation from a work, an important symbol, a character or a comparison of two characters, the author's style, his or her ideas about love, death, maturity, society, nature, money. You may wish to explore the author's use of names, choice of title, brand of humor. Suggestions for positions will be given with each assignment.

4. The paper must be your best writing. It will always be read by the instructor. At least two of your papers will be discussed and evaluated by the entire seminar.

5. Do not use the title of the work for your paper. Instead, your title should suggest or reflect your position.

6. Present your position logically and support it with concrete material—quotations and examples from what you have read as well as your own observations about life and literature. Don't neglect the plot or ignore the names of the characters, yet assume that your reader is your seminar classmate, who is also familiar with the work.

7. Writing good papers is hard work. It requires a clear outline. Your paper needs sharp first and last sentences, transitions between solidly developed paragraphs, varied sentences—not all beginning with pronouns, not all simple or compound constructions. It requires your sharpest and most mature language. Good writing is correct writing: don't lose your reader by failing to proofread. Read your paper aloud before typing the final draft. Finally, a good paper uses psychology: work hard on introductions and conclusions —the first and last things that the reader reads.

8. Do not rely on critics. While there will be student position papers for you to examine, take your own position.

9. Do not be afraid to adopt a position that seems "way out," fanciful, outrageous. If you have a strong position, one that may be challenged in the seminar discussion, just be sure that you have the material to defend it.

10. The writing of seven position papers is a cumulative experience. Each paper builds upon its predecessors, so do not hesitate to refer to previous papers or ideas—yours or those of other classmates. Through your own writing and by studying the works of other students, you will make discoveries about your reading and writing. New ideas will come to you. You will become aware of your own style as you consider the writing of others, especially Hemingway. And, while each paper will not necessarily be better than the last, your final production will speak for itself. You will be impressed!

PAPER I: "INDIAN CAMP"
DAYS 3–10

DAYS 3–5: READING THREE NICK ADAMS STORIES ALOUD

Goals

1. To introduce the Nick Adams stories by reading aloud and discussing on Day 3 "Up in Michigan" (1923) and "The Doctor and the Doctor's Wife" (1925); on Day 4 "The End of Something" (1925); and on Day 5 "The Three Day Blow" (1925).
2. To provide a background for an independent reading of "Indian Camp" (1925) and for writing the first Position Paper.

Materials

1. *The Short Stories of Ernest Hemingway*, which includes all of the short stories for Days 3–5.
2. *In Our Time*, which includes all but "Up in Michigan."

Assignment

1. Read "Indian Camp" and write a three-to-five-page Position Paper on that story.
2. Insert the DUE date for this paper on the Schedule. In addition, note the date of the first Defense Day and explain to students that copies of the position papers chosen for defense on that day will be given out on Day 16.

Procedure

1. Remind students that Hemingway's first published writings were about a young boy named Nick Adams, who, like Hemingway, went up to Michigan in the summer with his family. Suggest that the boy's name has been seen as symbolic, though you may not at this point want to deal with "Nick" (evildevil) and "Adams" (Adam of the Garden of Eden). Nevertheless, the Michigan landscape provided the setting for the awakening of a young innocent, a common theme in literature.
2. Read "Up in Michigan" aloud for immediate reaction. If you are uncertain about handling the sexual encounter between Jim and Liz, which may suggest certain parallels in the relationship between Nick and Marjorie, substitute an oral reading of "The Doctor and the Doctor's Wife," which appears after "Indian Camp" in *In Our Time*. Divide the story into sections of two or three paragraphs. Ask individual students to read a section aloud to the seminar; then summarize what they have read, observing whatever comes to mind about plot development, style, sentence length, dialogue, word choice, characters, names, the title, and the relationship of the story to Hemingway's life. Comment particularly on the relationship between Hemingway and his parents, the doctor-hunter father and the cultured Grace Hemingway who was not above using "illness" to get her way. It was his mother who insisted Ernest play the cello; it was his father who gave him his first gun.
3. As students read aloud these three stories on three consecutive days, they should begin to see the autobiographical nature of Hemingway's work, his emerging style, his use of the opening to mold the story, his ideas about what a boy learns. (What has Nick learned about his parents and himself in "The Doctor and the Doctor's Wife"? Why does Nick reject Marjorie yet accept the responsibility for hurting her? How does Nick's view of

life differ from Bill's in "The Three Day Blow"?) A question for you: Do the students relate readily to these stories? If not, what can you do to help them "connect"? A final question for the class: Suggest for each story at least one position that might be established in a three-to-five-page paper.

DAY 6: CHOOSING AND LIMITING TOPICS FOR POSITION PAPER I

Goals

1. To discuss appropriate topics for Position Paper I.
2. To demonstrate how to narrow a topic.

Materials

1. Handout 4: Suggestions for Position Paper I.
2. Handout 5: Student Model for Paper I.

Procedure

1. By now students have read "Indian Camp" and are beginning to understand Hemingway's early life and writing. Do not, however, discuss this story until *after* the position papers are handed in; but the concept of a position paper is probably incomplete and further clarification in class is needed.
2. Before suggesting suitable topics and how to narrow them, you may want to provide more background for the students. Useful sources:
    a. "Life" in Arthur Waldhorn's *A Reader's Guide to Ernest Hemingway,* pp. 6–10.
    b. "The High School Years" in Marcelline Hemingway Sanford's *At the Hemingways: A Family Portrait,* pp. 122–46.
    c. "The Michigan Years" and "Indian Camp" in Constance Cappel Montgomery's *Hemingway in Michigan,* pp. 11–18, 57–64.
    d. Carlos Baker, *Ernest Hemingway: A Life Story,* p. 160.
3. Distribute Handout 4 and discuss these suggestions for position papers on "Indian Camp." Since one of the suggestions deals with Hemingway's Code, his concept of "grace under pressure" in a world where ultimately one always loses, you will want to take time to develop this concept more fully.

The idea of the Hemingway Hero facing a hostile world with grace and courage will bear fruit throughout the seminar.

4. You may wish to use the model paper for "Indian Camp" at this point. You might post it on the bulletin board for student reference or make multiple copies for individual study. Note particularly the instructor's comments which follow the student paper.
5. If time remains, students should attempt to define individual positions, review the short story, and begin writing.

DAYS 7–10: COMPLETING PAPER I, READING, AND VIEWING A FILM

Goals

1. To provide in-class writing time for the completion of Paper I.
2. To read and discuss two additional Nick Adams stories: "Ten Indians" (1927), "The Battler" (1925), or "The Killers" (1927).
3. To view a film version of "My Old Man" (1923).

Materials

1. *The Short Stories of Ernest Hemingway.*
2. Film: *My Old Man* (color, 27 minutes), Encyclopaedia Britannica Educational Corporation. Note: a brief follow-up discussion by critics accompanies this excellent dramatization of the story.

Procedure

1. Days 7 and 8 should be used for in-class writing. Proofreading, a concept that must be developed throughout the semester, can be handled briefly on Day 9 before the papers are collected.
2. "Ten Indians," another initiation story set in Michigan, can be used for oral reading and discussion since it suggests that Nick is beginning to mature but still has the protective shell of "Indian Camp" that keeps his heart from being broken.
3. Paper I is due on Day 9 (Day 10 if you wish to allow more time). Allow time for a final proofreading before collecting the papers.

Students may then read aloud a final Nick Adams story. In either "The Battler" or "The Killers," an older, more independent Nick now encounters evil in new forms.

4. Choose the papers for Defense Day as soon as possible and make multiple copies. Review the Defense Day procedures in the introduction, The Seminar Method, in preparation for this discussion/evaluation period. The schedule allows time for you to grade the remaining papers before Defense Day (Day 17).

5. *My Old Man* is a superior film, beautifully acted with excellent timing. It retains the Hemingway ending that defies the formula story of mass media. Although the central character is named Joe, he is still Nick Adams, now abroad, finding life "funny" and puzzling. Students react immediately and intensely to the painful ending where the boy tries to find the truth in a world where "when they get started they don't leave a guy nothing." Suggestions for discussion: (a) List the names of the characters on the board and write a description of each. (b) Ask students what they know that Joe doesn't—about his father, about the prostitute. (c) Ask them about the title, its shades of meaning. Why did his father "betray" the gamblers, the bad guys? (d) What is Hemingway saying about life, about fathers and sons, about love (that pat on the knee on the train), about growing up? (e) Note that as in "Indian Camp" and "Ten Indians" no mother is present. Why does Hemingway leave the mother out?

HANDOUT 4
SUGGESTIONS FOR PAPER I: "INDIAN CAMP" (1925)

1. Consider the central character, the young Nick Adams. What is his function in the story? Why did Hemingway give him that name rather than Joe Smith or Archibald Beauchamp?

2. Note the title. The story is not called "Doctor and Son" but "Indian Camp." Why?

3. The story involves two groups: the whites on one side of the lake and the Indians on the other. What could this mean?

4. What is the function of Uncle George?

5. How do you see Nick's father—the wise scientist, the all-knowing father, the defeated man?

6. Hemingway believed in "grace under pressure," in living with reality in a world of pain, of good and bad luck. Who shows "grace under pressure" in this story?

7. Note Hemingway's style. Does any one aspect impress you? Why does he write in such short sentences? Why has he omitted the usual adverbs or other descriptions after the word "said"? Why does he use the variant name forms "Nick" and "Nickie," "Dad" and "Daddy"?

8. Use a key line or passage, such as the last two paragraphs, as the central idea for a position paper.

9. What is the meaning of the husband's suicide in the story?

10. Should the story have been longer? Should it, for example, have ended with the boy and his father returning home and discussing what had happened with Nick's mother?

11. Critic Arthur Waldhorn says that the Nick Adams stories are about "the terror of learning to live with the terrible." Is that what this story is about?

12. Hemingway was nearly killed in Italy during World War I. The theme of death haunted him for a lifetime. What does this story say about death?

HANDOUT 5
STUDENT MODEL FOR PAPER I

DIVIDED WE FALL

by Mark Champe

In his story "Indian Camp," Ernest Hemingway depicts the complex social interactions of the whites and Indians in Upper Michigan without seeming to take a definite stand. The segregation of the two groups is apparent from the beginning. To get to the Indians, the doctor and his son have to cross a bay. This suggests that the white and Indian settlements are far enough apart by land to make the boat trip practical. By separating them with water, Hemingway creates a much more vivid impression of the division than if he had put the Indian camp "just down the road" or on "the other side of town." The water acts as a social barrier as well as a geographical one. This is not to say that the barrier prevents a free flow of people between the two communities but rather that it constitutes a social fencing of the Indians by reducing their status. Those who are caged in are helpless; their status is automatically reduced by living in the camp and they cannot raise it while living there, but neither can they expect to go anywhere else and be accepted. They are far down the ladder.

Their physical separation as a group makes them more visible and less likely to be treated well by the majority. Throughout history, whenever one group of people is set off from the rest, either by its own choice or against it, social tensions between the two groups develop. The group in the majority likes having the minority in one place so they can be watched

1

2

easily and kept in line. Having them together also would eliminate the guilt feelings some members of the group might have about the mistreatment of the smaller group and would make their presence less difficult to accept. Any such feelings of guilt could be rationalized away by telling oneself that those in the minority are quite content with their own kind. This situation creates the impression of social balance, although the underlying requirements for producing it have a great potential for dissonance. When Uncle George gives cigars to the two Indians, it seems to be a friendly act. It is more of a reward for being "good boys" than a show of courtesy, more like giving a sugar cube to a horse than offering someone a cigar.

The effect of separation and consequent pseudo-balance is the steady dehumanizing and demoralizing of the minority. For this to work properly, the oppressors must be very careful to bring about their injustices as slowly as one would create a tolerance to poison, gradually increasing the dosage. The thing most counter-productive to the oppressor's cause is to aggravate the people enough to incite rebellion and possibly revolution. The United States today still might be a subservient colony of Great Britain had King George been more judicious with his levying of taxes. Fortunately for all of the would-be oppressed, this type of tyrannical equilibrium is very hard to attain because of the fairly strong human will.

The Upper Michigan example, however, comes quite close to this perfectly balanced imbalance. The stability of the system comes from the fact that the Indians don't seem to be on the verge of revolution, but rather they have arrived at a state in which their desperation is so great that they are completely insensitive to further action against them. When Uncle George is bitten in the arm by the Indian woman, he yells, "Damn squaw bitch!" Another Indian in the room just laughs at this, seemingly

3

not at all offended. This is a good example of what effective oppression
does to people. If the Indians had had any pride at all left, the least
response would have been a grim silence after the remark.

Another indication of the oppression is the decay of group soli-
darity. Had the Indian settlement existed before the white man came,
the difficult birth would be everyone's concern and everyone's pain.
The birth of a baby, especially a boy, was a very important event and if
it was not going well the whole community would be empathetic. Instead,
these Indians try as hard as they can to get out of range of the mother's
cries. Only an old woman, who may remember the pain of her own childbirth,
helps at all. The Indians still may have enough compassion to send for
the doctor, but that is about as far as it goes.

What gives meaning to the story is the way Hemingway presents the
two sides of the struggle. He never condemns either the whites nor the
Indians for being the cause or the maintainers of the problem. Some bad
and good points about each group are given, and the reader is left to
decide who is right. Hemingway doesn't preach by making the doctor evil
and the Indians good. The doctor is just a man who has found his own way
of dealing with what he feels is an unchangeable reality, and the Indians
are far from being saints. By examining the issues in the story, the
reader can better understand the extent to which racism is a problem and
why it probably will be around for some time to come.

Instructor's Comments

1. Strengths. This is a good first paper. The six paragraphs work
    together to define a clear and strongly personal position. More

4

sensitive than Hemingway's first readers were to civil rights, this student theorizes about social barriers and defines how Hemingway artistically defines racism in terms of the geography, plot, and language of this story. He relates literature to life.

2. <u>Weaknesses</u>. While the position is clear, the paper suffers from lack of extension. While the theorizing is more than adequate, undeveloped lines such as "Some bad and good points about each group are given" suggest that more specific details could be given to support the position.

PAPER II: "THE SUN ALSO RISES" DAYS 11-26

DAYS 11-12: BEGINNING A HEMINGWAY NOVEL

Goals

1. To orient students to *The Sun Also Rises* (1926).
2. To begin reading the novel in class.

Materials

Class set of *The Sun Also Rises* or *Three Novels: The Sun Also Rises, A Farewell to Arms, The Old Man and the Sea.*

Assignment

Note the DUE date of Paper II on the schedule.

Procedure

1. Remind students that the first Defense Day will be coming up in about five days. Copies of the papers for defense will be handed out the day prior to Defense Day. All papers will be returned at the end of Defense Day.
2. Ask students to review The Hemingway Chronology (Handout 2), noting that Hemingway has shifted to writing novels. *Torrents of Spring,* a minor work, was a parody of novelist Sherwood Anderson—a rather nasty publishing event since Anderson had befriended young Ernest, who was still an unknown. More can be said about this on Day 13. Pass out copies of *The Sun Also Rises* and help students to identify the names in the dedication (Hadley, the first wife; John or "Bumby," the first son).
3. *The Sun Also Rises* is a portrait of wounded people living in Paris, much as the wounded Hemingway did after serving as an ambulance driver on the northern Italian front in World War I. This book may seem slow to students ("Nothing really happens!"), but remind them that it shocked and intrigued the new generation of Americans who emerged from the high-blown idealism of the war. The style captures the mood of life in Paris. Ask students to note the biblical source (Ecclesiastes) of the title as well as the quote by Gertrude Stein, then living in Paris.
4. Before students begin reading, tell them that some students of Hemingway believe that the central character, Jake Barnes, is just Nick Adams, abroad and wounded.
5. Use the rest of Day 11 and all of Day 12 for in-class reading.

Additional Suggestions

1. Brief reference to maps of Paris, France, and Spain may be made at this point, as well as to books containing photographs of Hemingway at this time.
2. You may wish to use Hemingway's *A Moveable Feast,* pp. 11–31, to introduce Gertrude Stein ("Miss Stein Instructs") and to note Hemingway's scorn of the Lost Generation label ("Une Generation Perdue").

DAY 13: LEARNING ABOUT PARIS IN THE 1920s

Goal

To provide biographical, literary, and historical background for *The Sun Also Rises.*

Materials

Hemingway lived in Paris from 1921 to 1927, and numerous background accounts of the Paris expatriates are available. The following are readily obtainable and are suggested for background discussion and reading:

1. "Life" in Arthur Waldhorn's *A Reader's Guide to Ernest Hemingway,* pp. 10–14.
2. "Hemingway in Paris" in Malcolm Cowley's *A Second Flowering: Works and Days of the Lost Generation,* pp. 48–73.
3. Carlos Baker, *Ernest Hemingway,* pp. 153–55. A useful account of the background of the plot and title of *The Sun Also Rises.*

Procedure

1. Using maps, readings, and photographs, describe the excitement of Paris in the 1920s where life was inexpensive and culturally exciting for writers, painters, musicians (from Gertrude Stein to Picasso to George Gershwin)—a marked contrast to the more puritanical, Prohibition America. Paris was discovered by World War I soldiers, young Americans fed up with the slogans of the past. Expatriate writers especially gathered at Stein's salon to look at her collection of paintings, to discuss art and writing, to be free of Oak Park conventions. In Paris, Hemingway met a number of writers who influenced him: Ezra Pound, James Joyce, Sherwood Anderson, Stein, F. Scott Fitzgerald—the last three later getting rough treatment from Hemingway through parody, Anderson in *The Torrents of Spring* as a romantic primitivist, Stein in *A Moveable Feast* as a lesbian, Fitzgerald in *The Snows of Kilimanjaro* as a drunk.
2. For Hemingway, Paris meant writing as a reporter (note Cabelese in the Cowley chapter), living with Hadley and Bumby, losing his manuscripts (see the account in Baker, *Ernest Hemingway,* pp. 102–3), boxing, going to Sylvia Beach's book store (Shakespeare and Company), visiting the race track, traveling south to the bullfights in Pamplona and Madrid. Real people emerged as characters: Lady Duff Twysden as Lady Brett Ashley, Harold Loeb as Robert Cohn. In Paris, Ernest met Pauline Pfeiffer, and his first marriage fell apart.
3. Use maps to locate scenes in the novel as well as to identify important literary locations—the Left Bank, the Stein apartment at 27 rue de Fleurus, Notre Dame.

Additional Suggestion

Slides or resource persons (students if possible) can bring Paris alive. Even school-made slides from books on Paris and Hemingway can enliven the discussion and help students to visualize the locale of the novel.

DAYS 14–16: READING "THE SUN ALSO RISES" AND PREPARING FOR DEFENSE DAY

Goals

1. To provide time for students to continue reading *The Sun Also Rises.*
2. To prepare students for the first Defense Day.

Materials

Copies of the position papers on "Indian Camp" that you have chosen for the first Defense Day.

Procedure

1. Two full days, 14 and 15, will give students time to read a good portion of this medium-length novel. Hopefully, the previous discussion of life in Paris will motivate this reading.
2. On Day 16, hand out copies of the papers you have chosen for discussion on Day 17, the first Defense Day.
3. Encourage students to annotate their copies of these papers so that they will be able to remember their initial reactions to content and mechanics. Remind them that Defense Day is not Destruction Day. It is a time to learn about the positions of others, to clarify what is not clear, to agree and disagree, to study organization and supporting evidence, to work on mechanics, and to defend what one has written. The word "criticism" implies two responsibilities, for critics try to understand what a writer has written as well as to react to the writing.
4. Students whose papers have been chosen for Defense Day should prepare to read them aloud.

DAYS 17-18: PARTICIPATING IN DEFENSE DAY AND FOLLOW-UP

Goals

1. To conduct a first Defense Day that will provide a useful model for the remaining six.
2. To provide a follow-up that offers other students the opportunity to express their positions.
3. To help students examine the position of critics.

Materials

1. Extra copies of the position papers for students who may have lost or forgotten them.
2. Prior to class, review the discussion of how to conduct a successful Defense Day in the introduction, The Seminar Method. Write the three criteria for evaluating papers on the board: Clarity of Position; Organization and Support; Mechanics.
3. The corrected copies of the remaining position papers ready to give out at the end of the period.

Procedure

1. It is important that you choose good models for the first Defense Day and that you allot the discussion time equally. Remember, the students, not you, are to do the evaluating. Too much direction on your part will destroy the spirit of Defense Day; instead, encourage discussion, restate or clarify student positions, work for a balanced discussion (call on everyone, ask students who suggest grades to justify their choices), and conclude the defenses with positive summation. Always the goal is the next paper.
4. Return the other position papers at the end of the period without comment. The next class period will be given over to these papers.
5. Follow-up, Day 18, will allow others in the class to state their positions. There are a number of options for this day:
   a. Review the positions taken by the papers defended on the previous day. You may have taken notes on the positions of the remaining students and can, therefore, call on students who have similar or contrasting positions. Or each student can be called upon to state his or her position. Or you may ask other students to read all or selected portions of their papers—again, excellent models but ones not chosen for Defense Day.
   b. You may wish to discuss the successes (and failures) of the first Defense Day. Clear the air. Ask students how Defense Days can be improved. If some students argue that the grading was too high or too low, ask them to formulate a fair standard, taking into consideration the pressures of such close examination. Remind them that learning to write is more than just a letter grade.
   c. You may wish to read aloud a critic's evaluation of the Nick Adams stories or of "Indian Camp." Suggestions: (1) pages 27-33 of "Initiation Experiences" in Joseph DeFalco's *The Hero in Hemingway's Short Stories;* (2) "In Our Time: A Review" by D. H. Lawrence, pages 93-94, or portions of Philip Young's "Adventures of Nick Adams," pages 95-111, both in *Hemingway: A Collection of Critical Essays,* edited by Robert P. Weeks.

DAYS 19-22: SETTING THE SCENE FOR "THE SUN ALSO RISES" AND CHOOSING TOPICS FOR PAPER II

Goals

1. To provide background for and insight into the novel through films.
2. To suggest topics for Paper II.

Materials

1. Films: (a) *Hemingway's Spain: "The Sun Also Rises"* (color, 17 minutes), McGraw-Hill/ABC, 1969; (b) *Hemingway's Spain: "Death in the Afternoon"* (color, 15 minutes), McGraw-Hill/ABC, 1969.
2. Handout 6: Suggestions for Paper II.
3. Handout 7: Student Model for Paper II.

Procedure

1. The two films on Hemingway's Spain can be shown on whatever days they are available. Both are very fine films picturing the landscape of Spain, the setting of the novel, and bullfighting. Rod Steiger and Jason Robards narrate, using Hemingway's own words. The first film sets the scene of the novel; the second uses material from the 1932 nonfiction book on bullfighting but is excellent background for *The Sun Also Rises* since bullfighting is so important to its theme.
2. Time to complete the novel may be provided in class if necessary.
3. Handout 6 may be used in identifying positions for the second paper. The student paper for this assignment may be posted on the bulletin board for individual reference or copies made for distribution and discussion.

DAYS 23–24: READING ALOUD ANOTHER HEMINGWAY STORY

Goals

1. To read out loud "The Big Two-Hearted River" (1925) and to relate its theme to *The Sun Also Rises.*
2. To discuss Hemingway's style through "The Big Two-Hearted River."

Materials

Class copies of *The Short Stories of Ernest Hemingway.*

Procedure

1. Remind students that Hemingway took Nick Adams through a series of initiation experiences. Then, in 1925, he wrote "The Big Two-Hearted River," one of his most famous stories. The story tells of a wounded man who returns to Upper Michigan after World War I. The man is Nick Adams, not Nicky Adams. Nick is like the land he visits—burned out—and is looking for peace and quiet. Hemingway himself returned home to Oak Park a hero with medals, but then he too went back to his childhood summer home to recuperate and write. The story ties itself

to *The Sun Also Rises* in many ways—the wound, fishing, the search for oneself. It is famous for its style.
2. Ask students to read the story aloud by paragraphs, your role being to piece together the plot, comment on the style, encourage student reactions. The story is unforgettable and will influence students throughout the course (see Handout 19). Take the full two days.
3. You may want to read the account in Joseph DeFalco, *The Hero in Hemingway's Short Stories,* pp. 144–51.

DAYS 25–26: COMPLETING PAPER II AND READING A BACKGROUND STORY FOR "A FAREWELL TO ARMS"

Goals

1. To complete the writing and proofreading of Paper II.
2. To read "In Another Country" (1927) in preparation for *A Farewell to Arms.*

Materials

Copies of *The Short Stories of Ernest Hemingway.*

Procedure

1. Day 25 should be given over to writing and proofreading. Since students saw that proofreading errors detracted from the papers read on the first Defense Day, they will now be more concerned about careful proofreading.
2. Remind students that Paper II is due at the beginning of the period on Day 26. On that day the class should read aloud, without comments, "In Another Country," the genesis for *A Farewell to Arms,* Hemingway's next novel and the reading assignment on which Paper III will be based.
3. You may wish to preface the reading with Carlos Baker, *Ernest Hemingway,* p. 190, an account of how this story led to the novel. Again, refer to the map of Italy.
4. Immediately select the papers for the second Defense Day and have them reproduced. In-class time for grading the other papers is provided while the class goes on to read *A Farewell to Arms.*

HANDOUT 6
SUGGESTIONS FOR PAPER II: "THE SUN ALSO RISES" (1926)

1. Examine the quotations from Gertrude Stein and the Bible. Can one of these be developed? Perhaps you should do more background reading on Stein and the passages from Ecclesiastes.

2. The first words of the novel are "Robert Cohn." What is his function in the book? Should he be truly despised or is he the other side of Jake Barnes?

3. Is Hemingway a racist? Are his remarks about Jews and blacks evidence of prejudice?

4. Hemingway uses the word "funny" a good deal. What does this word mean in the book?

5. Consider Jake Barnes. Is he a hero, a man with "grace under pressure"? Or is he pathetic, an emasculated man?

6. Why is so much of the book about bullfighting and the fiesta?

7. Hemingway once said, "A writer's job is to tell the truth." What truth is he telling in this story?

8. Is this novel a love story? Why can't Brett and Jake fall in love and get married like characters do in romantic novels?

9. Why does Hemingway use the first-person narration in this novel?

10. What does Paris mean in this story? A beautiful, exciting city? A different city at night compared to the day?

11. Is Jake Barnes just Nick Adams grown up?

12. Hemingway is said to have a Code: a man must try to impose meaning where none seems possible, he must have courage and not quit, he must have discipline and control his death, he must behave with dignity. Is the Code in this novel?

13. Use a key line, such as the last one of the novel, for a paper.

14. What is the meaning of religion in this novel?

15. Some scholars say this is a topical novel, one about the 1920s and expatriates. If so, what does it say about them?

HANDOUT 7
STUDENT MODEL FOR PAPER II

THINGS THAT GO BUMP IN THE NIGHT

by Pat Chong

At night people find themselves, perhaps for the only time in their lives, alone, completely alone. The normal distractions of the day have gone home, to bed, or off the air, and all the reassuring objects of reality are hidden or rendered indistinct by the darkness. In the dark a person is left to confront himself, and he must do it honestly. The characters in The Sun Also Rises continually try, with varying degrees of success, to avoid facing themselves. Their primary methods of escape are drinking and being with their friends for most, or all, of the night. Still, none of them can totally avoid the effect of the night.

As Jake Barnes is the narrator of the story he is able to give a more detailed account of what influence the night has on him. At the start of the book it is night, and Jake is sitting in a cafe, then picks up a prostitute, attends a party, meets Brett, and then goes home. When he is with the prostitute, he tells her he is "sick," referring to his war wound. Later, while in the taxi with Brett he tells her, "What happened to me is supposed to be funny." Both times he refers to his wound; he does so in a matter-of-fact tone, seemingly jaded to the changes it has brought to his life. When alone in his apartment, he starts thinking about "the old grievance." In the dark Jake candidly examines his emotions:

> I try and play it along and just not make trouble for
> people . . . The Catholic Church had an awfully good way
> of handling all that . . . Not to think about it. Oh, it

1

2

was swell advice. Try and take it sometime. Try and take
it.

Jake acknowledges the power the night has over him. He says, "It is
awfully easy to be hard-boiled about everything in the daytime, but at
night it is a different thing." Jake repeats this philosophy later in
the book; then he says he did not sleep without a light on for six months.
He uses the past tense in the sentence to signify the fact that he is no
longer scared of the new perspective of life that the dark allows him to
see. As he is not as afraid anymore, he does not rely on alcohol to help
him avoid the effect of the night. He does stay up and observe his
friends trying to escape by drinking and being with other people.

The night plays a significant role in Brett's life. Initially, she
tries to avoid the night, but at the end of the book she also learns of
the importance of the night. In the beginning, Brett is able to show her
love to Jake only during the night, and even then she tries to avoid
expressing it. The first night Brett gets extremely drunk and allows a
count to pick her up; then she goes to see Jake, in the middle of the
night, leaving the count in the car waiting for her. To Jake she says,
"Just wanted to see you. Damn silly idea. Want to get dressed and come
down?" This statement reveals the battle that is going on inside her.
One side is fighting the night's effect on her; the other side is giving
in and telling him she wants to be with him.

A similar situation occurs the next evening when Jake, the Count,
and Brett dine together. She again becomes drunk. She offers to send
the Count away so they can be alone. Then later she tells Jake not to
kiss her and she will not see him again. Subsequently, she delays her
next encounter with Jake for three days by passing out on the train.
When she does meet up with him, she tries, once more, to avoid the night's

3

effect on her. She drinks and keeps her mind occupied with Mike Campbell and Pedro Romero. She is more successful this time as she fancies herself in love with Pedro. She confesses this to Jake while they take a nocturnal stroll. When she leaves Pedro, Brett shows her new understanding of how it is necessary to examine oneself carefully to be happy. During the meal she shares with Jake, she tells him not to get drunk, that it is not necessary. This reveals her new maturity since getting drunk was once her main way of combatting the dark. The final proof of her new awareness is in the last scene of the book. Brett rests against Jake in a taxi and says, "Oh, Jake, . . . we could have had such a damned good time together." This is said when it is "very hot and bright" outside, when daylight is at its strongest and Brett can openly admit her love. It is interesting to note that Brett and Jake at the start of the novel are in a cab at night where Brett asks Jake to kiss her and draws as far away as possible. At the end of The Sun Also Rises she knows the value of honestly facing up to herself. Brett will not fear the night again.

A symbolic incident involving Brett's growing awareness of the importance of the night occurs during her infatuation with Pedro. After a bullfight Pedro is awarded the ears of the bull, and he, in turn, gives them to Brett. She wraps them in Jake's handkerchief and places them, with several cigarette stubs, "far back" into her bed-table. The bed-table represents the night, and so everything she puts in it must be truthful. The stubs placed with the ears and handkerchief indicate that Jake and Pedro (in general, all men) are a vice to Brett, a fact established in the course of the book. Wrapping the ears with Jake's handkerchief shows Brett's desire to have both men in her life. That act also defines their separate roles. The ears are evidence of Pedro's skill in the arena, a major part of his allure, and so represent something

4

special and unique, yet also transitory. The handkerchief signifies Jake's role as a father figure, a protector. He is someone Brett always can go to for help. The symbolism is repeated in the novel. When Brett forces Pedro to leave, for the sake of his career, she turns to Jake for comfort.

Bill, a lesser character in the book, has a revealing discussion with Jake. While walking, they pass a taxidermist shop. Bill asks Jake if he wants a stuffed dog. Jake declines. Bill persists, saying, "[They] mean everything in the world to you after you bought it. Simple exchange of values. You give them money. They give you a stuffed dog." Bill expresses a certain cynicism. A dog symbolizes loyalty, friendship, trust, and blind love. Unfortunately, all these qualities are negated by the dog being stuffed. There is only the facade of these virtues. There is the suggestion that he has had a "stuffed dog" revealed to him, when he says they mean everything to the person who buys them. By bringing in money he degrades the value of the qualities a dog is supposed to possess. Later, he paraphrases a well known proverb: "Road to hell paved with unbought stuffed dogs." He equates stuffed dogs with good intentions. People's intentions, though seemingly good, really have no genuine inspiration. Finally, Bill confesses to have always loved stuffed animals. Again, this points to the fact that someone close to him may have been revealed as false. The nighttime brings Bill to the realization of human falsity, though alcohol helps him live with this understanding.

Mike appears to be the person most affected by the night. Three different times during the night he becomes drunk and attacks Cohn. The final time occurs in the evening of a foggy day. Mike, whom Jake describes as a "bad drunk," drinks to distort the view of life that night presents to him. His needling of Cohn, and to a lesser degree Pedro, shows that

5

at night Mike sees himself in a totally honest light, hating himself
because he always is bankrupt and cannot hold on to Brett. The alcohol
serves as an infuriator, an incentive to turn to other, weaker people,
and attack them to alleviate his self-hatred. Robert Cohn's fighting
back and knocking out Mike can be seen as Cohn's attempt to re-establish
some of his own ego. Mike and even Cohn use drinking as a safety valve
for releasing inner steam. Unlike the "good drunks," Bill and Brett,
they use the same tactics but fail because drinking for them is not an
escape mechanism.

All the characters in The Sun Also Rises to some extent try to avoid
facing themselves honestly. They reveal something of their character by
their method of escape, by their self-awareness in the night. Perhaps
when they hear things that go bump in the night, they are not so afraid
of their ghosts. They see that it is themselves knocking in their brains,
wanting to be recognized. Perhaps it is the fear of things that go bump
in the night that has driven them to escape into the world of alcohol, the
world of distorted images.

Instructor's Comments

1. Strengths. What a marvelous title! Not only has the author used it
    to suggest the paper's position but also to tie together the intro-
    duction, the conclusion, and all the concrete examples--the quotations,
    the four central characters--in her effort to defend a personal
    position. She has a sense of poetry, revealing to her classmates
    how a basic symbol was exploited in the novel and relating it as well
    to our own lives.

6

2. <u>Weaknesses</u>. While the paper may be flawed by wordiness, even by jerky sentences that do not always flow with each other, this first paper about a novel is ambitious and runs a full five pages. The reader cannot help but be sensitive to that ambition. You might point out the undocumented claim of the last paragraph that "all the characters" avoid themselves, but you should also help the seminar to appreciate the larger success of this paper.

PAPER III: "A FAREWELL TO ARMS" DAYS 27-42

DAY 27: BEGINNING TO READ HEMINGWAY'S MOST SUCCESSFUL NOVEL

Goals

1. To orient students to *A Farewell to Arms* (1929).
2. To provide in-class time to begin the novel.

Materials

Class copies of *A Farewell to Arms* or *Three Novels: The Sun Also Rises, A Farewell to Arms, The Old Man and the Sea.*

Assignment

1. Ask students to note the DUE date for the third paper on the Schedule, Day 42.
2. Remind students that Defense Day for Paper II *(The Sun Also Rises)* will be Day 34. Copies of the papers chosen for defense will be handed out on Day 33.

Procedure

1. Ask students to review The Hemingway Chronology (Handout 1), noting that the next book for consideration is the very successful *A Farewell to Arms.* At this time, Hemingway is re-examining his life and experiencing personal trauma. His first marriage has broken up, he has remarried and moved from Paris to Key West, Florida, where he will live for the next ten years. While he works on *A Farewell to Arms,* his father commits suicide back in Oak Park. The novel becomes a commercial success, establishing Hemingway's reputation as a writer of unusual style and a man sensitive to the agonies of war. Note the dedication to Gustavus A. Pfeiffer, the wealthy Arkansas uncle of his second wife, Pauline Pfeiffer, and a man who became a good friend, one of the first of the wealthy Pfeiffer clan to approve of Ernest.

2. Point out that the novel's title comes from a poem by the English writer George Peele (1558?-1597). Read the poem (see the *Oxford Book of Verse*) or post it on the bulletin board.

3. Explain that, although *A Farewell to Arms* is longer than *The Sun Also Rises,* its commercial success is partly explained by the fact that it has more of a plot and a greater sense of movement than the first novel. It has humor, memorable lines (turn, for example, to page 249 of the 1929 Scribner edition and note the lines beginning with "If people bring so much courage. . . ."), and strong symbols—such as the weather. Its title is a two-edged sword, referring to both love and war.

4. Ask students to begin reading the novel during the remainder of the class period.

DAYS 28-31: CONTINUING TO READ "A FAREWELL TO ARMS," SHARING RELATED HEMINGWAY SHORT STORIES, AND CHOOSING TOPICS FOR PAPER III

Goals

1. To provide in-class time for reading *A Farewell to Arms.*
2. To read aloud two related war stories—"Now I Lay Me" and "A Very Short Story"—both written in 1927.
3. To suggest topics for Paper III.

Materials

1. Class copies of *A Farewell to Arms.*
2. *The Short Stories of Ernest Hemingway.*
3. Handout 8: Suggestions for Paper III.
4. Handout 9: Student Model for Paper III.

Procedure

1. Use Days 28–29 for in-class reading of *A Farewell to Arms.*
2. Day 30 can be used for the oral reading of the two war stories ("Now I Lay Me" and "A Very Short Story") set in Italy that can be seen as background stories for the novel. Again, suggest how these stories remind us of Nick Adams growing up. DeFalco's *The Hero in Hemingway's Short Stories,* pp. 110–14, 162–63, is useful in preparing for the discussion.
3. During Day 31 suggest positions for Paper III, using Handout 8 as a point of departure. You may also wish to introduce the student model (Handout 9) at this point.

DAY 32: DISCUSSING WORLD WAR I AND THE HEMINGWAY BIOGRAPHY OF THIS PERIOD

Goals

1. To provide historical background for *A Farewell to Arms.*
2. To relate elements of the Hemingway biography to the novel.

Materials

A number of materials are useful for discussing World War I and Hemingway—maps, films, records, filmstrips. The following books are very useful:
1. "The Other War" in Malcolm Cowley's *A Second Flowering: Works and Days of the Lost Generation,* pp. 3–18, especially for literary background of the period.
2. Arthur Waldhorn's *A Reader's Guide to Ernest Hemingway,* pp. 14–16.
3. Leicester Hemingway's *My Brother, Ernest Hemingway,* pp. 97–100, on Hemingway in Key West and his father's death.
4. "It Was Great Fun" in James McLendon's *Papa: Hemingway in Key West, 1928–1940,* pp. 47–57, for backgrounds of the novel and the author's life at that time.
5. Carlos Baker's *Ernest Hemingway: A Life Story,* pp. 44–52, for a discussion of Hemingway's wound, his hospitalization, and his brief love affair with the prototype of Catherine Barkley—a nurse named Agnes von Kurowsky.

Procedure

1. Stress the fact that *A Farewell to Arms* is highly autobiographical; refer to Hemingway's own war wounds, his recuperation in Milan, his awful awareness that war was not like the stuff of the romantic novels that he had been raised on or jingoistic slogans (see Cowley, *A Second Flowering*), and his own love affair. In addition, the facts of Hemingway's life have their own death-in-life (the end of the love affair, the later dissolution of his first marriage, the death of his father by suicide, and even his wife Pauline's caesarian—note also "Indian Camp").
2. The novel is in microcosm the story of many young men and women who felt betrayed by the rhetoric of war when confronted by its realities. They, like Hemingway, were anxious to go "over there," wear fancy uniforms, and win medals. Other literary figures—Cummings, John Dos Passos, William Faulkner—eagerly enlisted in foreign organizations after the war began in 1914 and before the U.S. entered in 1917. They were the ones who later stayed in Paris and became part of the so-called Lost Generation.
3. Students will find much that is fascinating: Hemingway's awful wounds, his love affair, his return to Oak Park High School as a hero, his break with his parents after he goes up to Michigan to heal his psychic wounds ("The Big Two-Hearted River"). More can be said about this break on Day 37 when "Soldier's Home" is read out loud in class. Certainly the death of his father by suicide will spark discussion as to whether this event is related to Hemingway's own suicide.

DAYS 33–35: PREPARING FOR AND PARTICIPATING IN DEFENSE DAY AND THE FOLLOW-UP DISCUSSION

Goals

1. To provide additional in-class time for reading *A Farewell to Arms*.
2. To conduct a Defense Day and follow-up that offer students an opportunity to express and defend their positions.
3. To encourage students to look ahead to the third paper, accepting again the challenge of how best to present a well-documented position.

Materials

1. Copies of the papers you have chosen for Defense Day.
2. Corrected papers on *The Sun Also Rises* to return at the end of Defense Day.

Procedure

1. Day 33 is set aside for reading, though some students may use the class time to examine the position papers to be discussed during Defense Day.
2. Begin Day 34 by reviewing the Defense Day procedures, although the seminar should now be familiar with the system. Be sure to return all position papers on *The Sun Also Rises* at the end of the period.
3. During the follow-up discussion (Day 35), you might ask other students to read their papers for class comment, discuss the student paper (Handout 9), or present the viewpoint of a critic, e.g., "The Death of Love in *The Sun Also Rises*" by Mark Spilka in *Hemingway: A Collection of Critical Essays*, edited by Robert P. Weeks, pp. 127–38.

DAYS 36–42: COMPLETING THE NOVEL, DISCUSSING RELATED STORIES, AND WRITING PAPER III

Goals

1. To complete *A Farewell to Arms*.

2. To read and discuss in class two related stories, "Soldier's Home" (1925) and "Fathers and Sons" (1933).
3. To provide class time to write and revise Paper III.

Materials

Copies of *The Short Stories of Ernest Hemingway*.

Procedure

1. Days 36–38 should provide enough time to complete the novel and to read aloud "Soldier's Home." The story suggests Hemingway's state of mind as he returned home to Oak Park (though the young man is Krebs and he returns to Oklahoma) and correlates well with *A Farewell to Arms*. The piece is a marvelous artifact of the 1920s and may also be used to discuss Hemingway's emerging style (especially the idea of repetitions taught him by Gertrude Stein). The story also suggests Hemingway's break with his parents that took place in Michigan. You may wish to supplement this discussion with material from Constance Cappel Montgomery's *Hemingway in Michigan*, pp. 172–82, or Carlos Baker's *Ernest Hemingway*, pp. 56–74.
2. Days 39–41 should be used for writing, revising, and proofreading the third paper.
3. Use Day 42 to read out loud "Fathers and Sons," a story which makes an interesting transition between the war novel and the grown-up Nick Adams, now an author (with a son—Bumby) who is reflecting on his father's suicide—all materials related to Hemingway's own life. This last of the Nick Adams stories brings that part of Hemingway's writing career to an end. It is also a very moving story of a mature Hemingway, no longer so resentful of his parents (as in "Soldier's Home") and now aware of his own mortality, of being a father as well as a son. The prose is more mature as well, not so experimental, though there is the familiar Hemingway description of nature, the sharp dialogue, the repeat of earlier Nick Adams

plots, and an awareness of life that high school students understand (cf. "My Old Man"): life must be learned; not everything can be taught, especially intense experiences such as Nick's childhood sexual encounter.

4. Collect the third Position Paper on Day 42. Select the papers for the next Defense Day and have them reproduced.

Additional Suggestion

The film version of "Soldier's Home" (see Bibliography) can be excellent for comparison with the actual short story.

HANDOUT 8
SUGGESTIONS FOR PAPER III: "A FAREWELL TO ARMS" (1929)

1. Consider the title. Does it have more than one meaning? Use the poem, too.
2. Is this a war novel, a romantic novel, or what?
3. The weather seems to play an important role in this novel. What do the various types of weather mean, especially the rain?
4. Is Lieutenant Henry another Code Hero? Are his flight from the war and his seeming coldness at the end of the novel symptoms of a Hero gone wrong?
5. What is the function of Rinaldi in the novel?
6. Is Catherine a rounded character or a stick figure? Does Hemingway understand women?
7. Does Hemingway have a sense of humor in this novel? If so, what kind of humor does he use?
8. Try a contrast paper: Jake Barnes and Lieutenant Frederic Henry.
9. What is the function of the first-person narration?
10. This might be the time to do some research. Is this novel more biography than fiction?
11. Why did Hemingway kill off Catherine Barkley in childbirth? Does anyone remember Thornton Wilder's *Our Town?*
12. What is the truth in this novel? Look at page 249 again, especially the line: "The world breaks every one and afterward many are strong at the broken places."
13. What about religion in this novel? Why does Henry pray?
14. What is the function of food in the novel?
15. While Hemingway was revising his first draft of this novel, his father committed suicide. Can you tie these two events together?

HANDOUT 9
STUDENT MODEL FOR PAPER III

ADOLESCENCE TO ADULTHOOD

by Melody Myers

Ernest Hemingway's characters are strong individuals, but he was inclined to build his characters with similar dispositions and reactions. Nick Adams of "Indian Camp" and Frederic Henry of A Farewell to Arms endured a similar situation and reacted to it as if they were the same person. Instead of the innocent onlooker that was Nick, Henry became painfully involved and a sufferer of life. They shared the same responses, but a change can be detected from Nick the boy to Henry the man. The difference between the two is that Henry represents a matured Nick Adams.

Nick's first unpleasant exposure to the Indian camp was to observe a screaming Indian woman who had been in labor for two days but was still unable to give birth to her child. The purpose of his father's trip to the camp was to deliver the child. The doctor examined the woman and concluded that a Caesarian section must be performed to give relief to the mother and child. Nick's primary concern was the woman's screaming. He even inquired if his father could stop her agony of pain.

> "Oh, Daddy, can't you give her something to make her stop screaming?" asked Nick.
> "No. I haven't any anaesthetic," his father said.

Henry also was confronted with a woman in childbirth. The woman was his lover, Catherine. The situation was more personal and emotional than Nick's, yet concern was shared by both. When complications occurred and Catherine began screaming, Henry tried to comfort her by giving her gas. Henry said, "I'll make it [the gas] work. I'll turn it all the way."

1

2

Like Nick, Henry wanted to relieve the pain of childbirth. Yet the possibility that too much gas could result in death worried Henry. Catherine's apparent suffering finally took priority over death.

In "Indian Camp," Nick had the opportunity to watch his father perform a Caesarian operation. Even though Nick held the basin for his father during the procedure, he preferred not to watch. In fact, after Dr. Adams invited Nick to observe him as he put in the stitches, Nick did not watch. "His curiosity had been gone for a long time." Apparently Nick had his fill of childbirth. He had already endured more than what he had anticipated.

Catherine's doctor also decided that a Caesarian section was the easiest and safest way to relieve both the mother and child. Henry was given the same chance to observe a Caesarian operation as had Nick.

> "You can go in the other door and sit up there," a nurse
> said to me [Henry]. There were benches behind a rail that
> looked down . . . at Catherine. The mask was over her face
> and she was quiet now. They wheeled the stretcher forward.
> I turned away and walked down the hall.

Henry also passed up the chance of medical observation. His sense of responsibility and guilt were too much for him. As much as he hated to face the truth, he knew that Catherine was paying the consequences for loving him. He hated it all, but later he returned to the operating room to watch the doctors sew up the incision. Henry thought, "I do not think I could have watched them cut, but I watched the wound closed into a high welted ridge with quick skillful-looking stitches like a cobbler's, and was glad." Henry, unlike Nick, enjoyed watching the final part of the operation. The completion of the surgery proved the first step of Catherine's recovery. The final stitches seemed to verify the ending of a traumatic ordeal. Now that the baby had been delivered, it was only logical that Catherine's recuperation would follow.

3

On the trip home from the Indian camp, Nick and his father discussed the pain of childbirth, suicide, the difference between male and female suicides, and death itself. Too early in life, Nick had seen too much suffering. This had been Nick's initiation to pain, to the violence of birth and death. The story concluded, "In the early morning on the lake sitting in the stern of the boat with his father rowing, he felt quite sure he would never die." After experiencing the unpleasantness of birth and death, Nick refused to accept them as part of reality. In returning home he concluded that he would never die. Childish? Perhaps. But that was what he believed. By rejecting the pain he had seen and felt, Nick thought he could avoid death forever. He was trying to cope with life, the burden of adulthood. He had shouldered more than what he was ready to carry. At one time or another, a young man may think he shall never die. It is easier for a young man to stand by and watch, for he is not yet painfully involved; he is not a sufferer, only an onlooker. Rather than swallow the truth about childbirth and death, Nick Adams justified them to suit himself.

Lt. Henry found himself confronted with the violence of birth and death, too. Facing reality did not come easy for Henry either. He realized the seriousness of Catherine's operation, but the possibility of her death was unacceptable.

> Yes, but what if she should die? She won't die. She's just having a bad time. . . . Afterward we'd say what a bad time and Catherine would say it wasn't really so bad. But what if she should die? . . . She can't die. Yes, but what if she should die? She can't, I tell you. Don't be a fool. . . . It's just nature giving her hell.

Henry had his doubts as to whether or not Catherine would live, but he loved her and he tried to avoid the likelihood of her death. Henry's reaction was human. Nobody wants loved ones to die. Rather than confronting the alternatives of what could happen, Henry justifies Catherine's

4

complications as "nature giving her hell." He felt that Catherine's suffering would end when "nature" decided to let her go from the grip of hell. He implied it was only a matter of time before Catherine would be relieved from her agony of pain. His justification gave him the hope he needed.

In "Indian Camp," Dr. Adams tells Nick, fathers "are usually the worst sufferers in these little affairs [childbirth]." Frederic Henry was the father of Catherine's child; he had suffered. Henry was numb from death, not from fears for himself--like Nick Adams, but from the loss of his lover. Henry had seen death in war, but it had never touched him the way this single death would for the rest of his life.

As a boy, Nick Adams had a hard time accepting reality. He could not look at life objectively because he had not lived life. Henry also tried to take life in stride, but obstacles got in his way. Henry has experienced war, death, love. He had lived life. Therefore, accepting life's consequences was easier for him as an adult than it was for Nick as an adolescent. Nevertheless, Henry was not untouched by life's misfortunes because memories would be with him forever. His pain was real and lasting. Instead of avoiding the facts of life as Nick Adams has done, Frederic Henry had confronted reality face to face and accepted it for what it was.

Instructor's Comments

1. Strengths. This student tackled a difficult writing problem, comparing two characters from different works. She is sensitive to balance, to concrete documentation, and to the development of her position about the different perceptions of a boy and a man. Beneath the prose is her understanding of Hemingway's maturing concept of life and death. I also think she is reflecting about her own

5

maturity. In this writing design, she has obviously worked on organizational structure, if not on ways to integrate direct quotations into the text.

2. <u>Weaknesses</u>. While considerable effort was given to structure and the use of concrete illustration, this paper can be seen as somewhat flawed by its lack of sentence variety, a writing goal for Paper III. Many of the paragraphs are stitched together with simple and compound sentences, often beginning with a character's name or a pronoun.

PAPER IV: A PROFILE OF ERNEST HEMINGWAY DAYS 43–57

DAY 43: REVIEWING THE HEMINGWAY BIOGRAPHY AND INTRODUCING THE PROFILE PAPER

Goals

1. To review the Hemingway biography in broad outline.
2. To orient students to Paper IV, a profile of Ernest Hemingway.

Materials

1. Assemble a class library of biographical and autobiographical materials (see Bibliography).
2. Handout 10: Suggestions for Paper IV.
3. Handouts 11 and 12: Student Models for Paper IV.

Assignment

1. Ask students to note the DUE date for Paper IV on the Schedule, Day 57.
2. Paper IV should be based on at least one hundred pages of reading from nonfictional materials about or by Hemingway. The one hundred pages may be taken from a single source or from several sources. A bibliography and footnotes are required.

Procedure

1. In explaining the assignment, remind students that they may use the fictional writings of Hemingway previously read in class but that this material may not be counted toward the one hundred pages of reading required for the Profile Paper.
2. Distribute copies of the model papers for this assignment for subsequent discussion by the class.
3. Before considering ideas for the Profile Paper, review The Hemingway Chronology and place the following outline on the board:

I. The Early Years, 1899–1921. Growing up in Oak Park (family, high school), summers in Michigan, Kansas City *Star* reporter, ambulance driver in Italy in World War I, reporter for the Toronto *Star,* marriage to Hadley.

II. The Paris Years, 1921–1927. Foreign correspondent, life among the expatriates (Stein, Pound, Fitzgerald, Anderson, Joyce), literary success, birth of Bumby, bullfighting, divorce and remarriage (Pauline Pfeiffer).

III. The Key West Period, 1927–1940. Interest in deep sea fishing, purchase of the *Pilar,* birth of Patrick and Gregory, Africa and big game hunting, father's suicide, literary support of Loyalists in Spanish Civil War, divorce by Pauline and marriage to Martha Gellhorn, move to Finca Vigia near Havana.

IV. The World War II Period, 1940–1945. Sub chaser in Caribbean, war correspondent, "liberator" of Paris, divorce from Martha and marriage to Mary Welsh.

V. The Cuban Period, 1945–1960. Critical attack on *Across the River and into the Trees,* death of mother, publication of *The Old Man and the Sea* in *Life,* Nobel Prize, purchase of Ketchum, Idaho, hunting lodge, work on memoirs.

VI. Ketchum, Idaho, and the End. Beginning of breakdown, hospitalization in Rochester, Minnesota, death from self-inflicted gunshot wound.

4. Distribute Handout 10 (Suggestions for Paper IV) for previewing now and for reference later.

5. Encourage students to examine the class collection of Hemingway materials and to seek out materials in libraries. You may wish to distribute copies of portions of the Bibliography.

Additional Suggestions

1. You may wish to use the filmstrip-tape *Ernest Hemingway* in The American Experience in Literature: Five Modern Novelists, available from the Encyclopaedia Britannica Educational Corporation. See the Bibliography for this and other filmstrip/record-cassette suggestions.
2. The seminar may wish to contact resource persons through, for example, the Bell Telephone leased phone system (see Appendix A). Those who knew Hemingway or know much about him, such as college English professors, may be willing to be interviewed by seminar members.

DAYS 44–48: LOCATING AND SHARING A HEMINGWAY ANECDOTE WITH THE CLASS

Goals

1. To help students locate interesting biographical information about Hemingway.
2. To provide a range of anecdotal material that will help students choose a biographical focus for Paper IV.

Materials

1. Class library, supplemented by student research.
2. Film: *Hemingway*, 54 minutes.
3. Seven Anecdotes from the Hemingway Biography (Appendix C).

Assignment

1. Ask each student to find one concrete anecdote about Ernest Hemingway to share with the class. (See the seven anecdotes in Appendix C.)
2. Anecdote days (47–48) should help to trigger a position. A single anecdote may be used by a given student as the basis for a profile paper or several anecdotes along a similar line may suggest a tactic. Encourage students to use each other's anecdotes and to share source materials.

Procedure

1. Show the excellent documentary film on Hemingway's life on Day 44. If the film is not available, you might use the filmstrip-tape suggested for Day 43 or a slide show made from photographs on Hemingway's life prepared by your school's A-V department.
2. On Day 45, announce the anecdote assignment. While some students may be capable of independent research, others may require a more directed approach. The following suggestions will simplify the assignment and help to ensure that all students find interesting "slice-of-life" anecdotes. A retelling of the first seven anecdotes is included in Appendix C.
   a. Boxing in Paris: Carlos Baker, *Ernest Hemingway: A Life Story*, pp. 22–23; Morley Callaghan, *That Summer in Paris*, pp. 97–100, 118–22.
   b. A childhood accident: Leicester Hemingway, *My Brother*, pp. 19–22.
   c. Hadley loses manuscripts: Carlos Baker, *Ernest Hemingway: A Life Story*, pp. 102–3.
   d. Key West, at Sloppy Joe's, fishing: Leicester Hemingway, *My Brother*, p. 164; McLendon, *Papa*, pp. 152–53.
   e. Punches poet Wallace Stevens: McLendon, *Papa*, pp. 55–57.
   f. African air crashes: Carlos Baker, *Ernest Hemingway: A Life Story*, pp. 518–22.
   g. Suicide attempts: Leicester Hemingway, *My Brother*, p. 256; Carlos Baker, *Ernest Hemingway: A Life Story*, pp. 199, 554–64; A. E. Hotchner, *Papa Hemingway: A Personal Memoir*, pp. 264–304.
   h. Average workday, Sloppy Joe's: McLendon, *Papa*, pp. 145–48.
   i. Fitzgerald referees a Hemingway boxing match: Callaghan, *That Summer in Paris*, pp. 209–13.

j. Ernest wants father's suicide gun: Leicester Hemingway, *My Brother*, pp. 98–100.
k. Hemingway discovers new writing technique: Carlos Baker, *Ernest Hemingway: A Life Story*, pp. 525–29.
l. Hotchner's last talk with Ernest: Hotchner, *Papa Hemingway*, pp. 296–300.
m. Mary and Ernest Hemingway meet, fight: Mary Hemingway, *How It Was*, pp. 121–31.
n. Winning the Nobel Prize: Carlos Baker, *Ernest Hemingway: A Life Story*, pp. 525–29. (Note: here the student or instructor may wish to use the record or tape *Ernest Hemingway Reading*, available from Caedmon, which includes his reading of his Nobel Address.)

3. Share and discuss the anecdotes on Days 47–48. You may wish to bring an anecdote to share, too. Remind students that the research reading for anecdote day should help to locate material for Paper IV; the shared anecdotes should also provide a pool of biographical information for the class to draw upon in writing the Profile Paper.

DAYS 49–51: PREPARING FOR AND PARTICIPATING IN DEFENSE DAY AND FOLLOW-UP

Goal

To help students refine their understanding of how a position becomes warranted through clear argumentation and adequate documentation.

Materials

1. Copies of the papers you have chosen for Defense Day.
2. Corrected papers on *A Farewell to Arms* to return at the end of Defense Day.

Procedure

1. Use Day 49 for research reading for Paper IV or for the study of the position papers to be used on Defense Day.

2. Follow the Defense Day procedures outlined earlier. Return all papers at the end of the period.
3. Use the follow-up day to discuss the papers of other students, to evaluate the student models (Handouts 11 and 12), or to consider a critic's point of view, e.g., "Loser Take Nothing" by Philip Young in *20th Century Interpretations of "A Farewell to Arms,"* edited by Jay Gellens, pp. 28–32.

DAY 52: LEARNING ABOUT "NADA" THROUGH READING ANOTHER HEMINGWAY STORY

Goals

1. To read out loud "A Clean Well-Lighted Place" (1933) and to relate its theme to other Hemingway works and to the Hemingway biography.
2. To discuss the concept of *Nada*, an important term in Hemingway criticism.

Materials

Copies of *The Short Stories of Ernest Hemingway*.

Procedure

1. At this point, introduce the concept of *Nada* through "A Clean Well-Lighted Place." This idea will appear in the biographical and critical reading being done by students for Paper IV and will add a new dimension to their understanding of Hemingway's Code Heroes.
2. Read the story aloud, asking students to take turns reading and reacting. The relatively negligible plot deals with Hemingway's poetic vision of despair—perhaps darkest in this story—of people trying to find meaning in a world where none is possible. The story reminds us that the lights go out for everyone, and thus the parody of the Lord's Prayer. Yet all people "need a light for the night." (See pages 27–29 in Waldhorn's *A Reader's Guide to Ernest Hemingway*.)
3. Use the remaining time for research reading for Paper IV.

DAYS 53–57: COMPLETING PAPER IV AND READING TWO MORE HEMINGWAY STORIES

Goals

1. To give students time in class to write, revise, and proofread the Profile Paper.
2. To read out loud "A Day's Wait" (1933) and "The Old Man at the Bridge" (1938).

Materials

Class copies of *The Short Stories of Ernest Hemingway*.

Procedure

1. Day 53 is the final reading and research day for Paper IV. On Day 54 students begin work on rough drafts of the Profile Paper, completing revisions and proofreading on Days 55 and 56.
2. The Profile Position Paper is due on Day 57. You may wish to schedule two Defense Days so that all students will have defended at least one paper before Paper VII, the Summation Paper. At this point, inform the class that something *different* will be done on Defense Day for the last paper. Do not, however, discuss Paper VII at this time. The number of papers you select for the fifth and sixth Defense Days will, of course, depend upon the number of students in your seminar.
3. After collecting the profile papers, read aloud two very short stories. "A Day's Wait" is an amusing story about a boy who thinks he is dying but isn't. The story has biographical overtones: in 1932, the Hemingways were in Arkansas visiting Pauline's relatives when Bumby came down with the flu and a temperature of 102. In this story, the boy's sudden maturity and then retreat back to childhood are of special interest. "The Old Man at the Bridge," set on an Easter Sunday during the Spanish Civil War, not only suggests Hemingway's personal involvement in that struggle, but also lends itself to a discussion of his theme and style—the irony of a man with no hope on a dry, desolate day compared to Christ's Easter, the use of animals (who have instinct), the awfulness of innocence caught up in human evil, the symbol of the bridge, the central character without a name.
4. Select and reproduce papers for the coming Defense Day.

HANDOUT 10
SUGGESTIONS FOR PAPER IV: THE PROFILE PAPER

1. Can any one of the readings define a narrowed theme? For example, is Morley Callaghan's observation about Hemingway and boxing related to what you have read?

2. Try to synthesize Hemingway the man into a single word. What would it be? Then expand upon how Hemingway meets the definition of that word.

3. Who taught Hemingway? Can you name three teachers? How did they mold him?

4. Hemingway had four wives. Were they at all alike? Why would a boy from a proper Oak Park, Illinois, background lead such an unconventional life?

5. Is there a key event in Hemingway's early life that did a great deal to shape him, for example, his World War I injury?

6. Is Hemingway a male chauvinist?

7. Do the early writing and biography suggest that Hemingway would later commit suicide? Was his suicide consistent with his Code and his writing?

8. Hemingway loved boxing, fishing, hunting, the out-of-doors. Why?

9. Can you find a Hemingway quotation that seems to define him and his writing?

10. Was Hemingway a disciplined writer? If so, how would you define and illustrate his "discipline"?

11. Would you like to have been a friend or relative of this famous man and writer?

12. Ernest Hemingway seemed entranced with bullfighting. Why?

13. Relate Hemingway to Nick, Jake, and Frederic. Are they his mouthpieces?

14. Do some research on a friend that Hemingway later rebuffed (Gertrude Stein, F. Scott Fitzgerald, Sherwood Anderson). How do you explain the break?

15. Was Hemingway an American or a citizen of the world, a kind of man without a country? What values did he hold?

HANDOUT 11
STUDENT MODEL FOR PAPER IV: USE OF BIOGRAPHY

THE ROMANCE AND TREACHERY OF HEMINGWAY'S EGO

by Dan Goldberg

Celebrity status in America has traditionally been reserved for performers and athletes. Occasionally, political or social registers may spawn such superstars, but only one author has ever attained such prestige: Ernest Hemingway. Hemingway is the only American writer of modern times whose fame has exceeded his literary accomplishments. He is the most biographed, talked about, romanticized author in our literary heritage.

Hemingway's own energies were responsible for making him such a newsworthy item. He was in constant motion, in public view, whirling from one romantic stage to another. Everything he did was bigger than life. For the press, he was a perpetual drama, always good for a scoop. After Hem's death, Hemingway constituted the walls of a fort: Hemingway had given the power to believe that he could still shout down the corridors of a hospital, live next to the breath of the beast, accept his portion of dread each day. Yet the greatest living romantic was also mortal.

The motivating force in Hemingway's life, that which made him so romantic, was his own insatiable ego. He continuously sought ways to assert his masculine independence. There was never a time when he was not battling to prove himself. Most of the battles were waged from within, for he rarely had trouble obtaining the respect of his peers.

Hemingway's reputation as a double-crosser was a result of such self-liberating impulses. Whenever he felt a benefactor edging in, a

1

2

friend expecting thanks, he pulled the rug from beneath them. Sherwood
Anderson was a classic example of this kind of treatment. He had championed
Hemingway's work and even helped the younger author to obtain a publisher.
The two men had been friends for a number of years when Ernest decided to
do his number on him. Hemingway devoted an entire book, The Torrents of
Spring, to satirizing Anderson. He even had the gall to send it to
Anderson's own publisher. This came at a time when Anderson was a hot
item and considered to be Ernest's mentor. Ernest hated this. It withered
his sense of independence. And that is why he attempted to mangle Anderson's reputation and dissociate himself from any previous connection he had
with the author of Winesburg, Ohio.

The Torrents of Spring was not an entirely undeserved attack. There
are some indications that Anderson was taking credit for some of Hemingway's
style. That kind of thing was just enough to tousle Ernest's pride and
ignite his paranoic ego. He always wanted to give the impression that
everything he had was self-acquired, particularly his writing. Anderson
was hurt by Hemingway's over-reaction, but he might have had some of it
coming to him.

Gertrude Stein had a similar relationship with Hemingway, and she too
got hers in the end. In his early years in Paris in the 1920s, Ernest
spent a good deal of time in Stein's apartment, enjoying her company and
art collection. They had a close relationship professionally as well as
socially. He often consulted her about his work and greatly respected her
advice. Yet, when she began to close in on Hemingway, the ax fell upon
her also. There was method in this attack. Stein was a powerful personality and demanded a certain amount of conformity from her friends,
yet Hemingway's rebellion seems particularly cruel. Much later, in A
Moveable Feast, he went so far as to insinuate that she was a lesbian.
Ironically, this attack was published long after she died.

3

Hemingway always resorted to dramatic measures to cut his imagined
apron strings. He violated Stein's friendship with many personal barbs
that deliberately cut deep. In retrospect, his attack seems to have come
almost spontaneously. One moment he was congenial and then suddenly he
turned ferocious, a type of behavior that repeated itself many times
throughout Ernest's life, especially after he had lived in one place for
a stretch of time. When he wasn't free to roam, he thirsted for a
collision.

While writing, Hemingway also seemed to be battling. Once he had
attained a degree of success, he often went to war with his critics. From
the time of For Whom the Bell Tolls (1940) to the appearance of The Old
Man and the Sea (1952), every piece he published had a challenge to go
with it. He loved to rage over reviews, for it gave him a chance to prove
himself over and over. He all but declared himself king of contemporary
American literature and glorified in his fights with pretenders to the
throne.

The Hemingway legend is packed with stories of fist fights and
bloodied noses. The image of himself in constant combat was food for his
ego. He could obtain no final victory, for such an event would leave him
with nothing to do. For Ernest, writing--as life itself--was an endless
marathon. Yet a person had to continue as if a finish was in sight.
"They can't yank novelists like they can pitchers," Hemingway would stutter.
"A novelist has to go the full nine, even if it kills him" (Ross, 1962,
p. 18). Even if it kills him. In Ernest's case, it had to kill him.
Otherwise he would not have gone the full nine. Pride dictates that there
is always another battle to be won. There was never a final victorious
battle in his own ego war. One conquest merely led to the next. He said,

4

> It is sort of fun to be fifty and feel you are going to
> defend the title again. . . . I won it in the twenties and
> defended it in the thirties and the forties, and I don't
> mind at all defending it in the fifties. (Ross, 1962, p.
> 28)

Hemingway put his pride on the line with every new book. He devoured every triumph and never acknowledged defeat. In his own mind, every novel was a prize fight, a championship, standing proof that he still could pack a knockout punch. When he lost that punch, it was over for him. An ego of his size could not reconcile the fatigues of turning sixty. He felt his body going bad and his words drying up. There were no more titles to defend. Therein lies the reason for his suicide.

Ernest's last few months were spent in misery. He was in and out of the Mayo Clinic for mental and physical examinations. Doctors perforated his brain with electric shocks, mechanical stimulants to exercise his titanic depression. Or maybe they were futile attempts to poke air holes in his suffocating ego.

The outdoor world, which had tantalized Hemingway practically since his birth, now turned gray on him. What good were the beauties of nature if there was no way to describe them? The words wouldn't "come any more," and he grew thinner and weaker and more depressed.

There was no way for a man of Hemingway's beliefs to grow old gracefully. In Hemingway's vernacular, the day you could no longer write was the day you died. There was no "old" in the Hemingway ego system. When he created, he was forever young; when he could no longer fight the battle, he was done. There was no middle ground. He set about single-mindedly to kill himself.

It could be said that he died of strangulation, murdered by his own pride. He had always carried his own ego like a beast upon his back. When it was well fed, it was docile; as it grew hungry, it was murderous.

5

His majestic pride gave him the desire to create. It had been glossy and glowed like the sun before the public. But the sun also must set, says Ecclesiastes, Hemingway's only bible, and his unsatisfied ego took back its gift.

After such a richly dramatic life, his death was painstakingly simple. He put two bullets in his head and that was all. Death was the very end; he had always made that clear. There was no need for romance afterward. And there are not chronicles of utter grief at Ernest's funeral. Those that understood him knew there was no reason for it. When the end came, he had done all he could do. He had splurged lifelong on pleasures that took their physical toll. His soul had been wrung for all the lessons it could give the world, so there was no more left there either. Despite his sovereign ego, Hemingway was a mortal man. He had reached his limitations.

Bibliography

Baker, Carlos. Ernest Hemingway: A Life Story. New York: Scribner's, 1969.

Keats, John. You Might As Well Live: The Life and Times of Dorothy Parker. New York: Simon and Schuster, 1970.

Mellow, James. Charmed Circle: Gertrude Stein and Company. New York: Praeger, 1974.

Ross, Lillian. "How Do You Like It Now, Gentlemen?" in Hemingway, edited by Robert P. Weeks. Englewood Cliffs, N.J.: Prentice-Hall, 1962.

Instructor's Comments

1. Strengths. This is a strong position paper, one that is not interested in a balanced profile. The student has been to Roget and back; he is well read, he knows how to use language and anecdote. This paper will

6

stimulate any seminar and may irritate some instructors ("she too got hers in the end"). It brings to flesh the cold facts of most high school reference books.

2. Weaknesses. The startling generalizations ("There was no middle ground") and the dramatic prose ("his suffocating ego") often seem more personal than documented. While the bibliography is there, the footnotes are missing. Perhaps the paper would have been more convincing if one situation, such as his relationship with Sherwood Anderson, had been exploited in depth.

HANDOUT 12
STUDENT MODEL FOR PAPER IV: COMBINING USE OF BIOGRAPHY AND LITERATURE

THE ULTIMATE QUESTION

by Amy Freeman

> He was a man of prowess and did not want to live without
> it: writing prowess, physical prowess, sexual prowess,
> drinking and eating prowess. . . . But if he could only be
> made to adjust to a life where these prowesses were not
> so all important. . . .
>
>   A. E. Hotchner, 1961

But he would not adjust. During his last days at Ketchum, Idaho, and Rochester, Minnesota, Ernest Hemingway finally completed the ideas which his characters had implied throughout his works. Through the action and the feelings that he exhibited during this time, he composed his final plot: a plot which answered the essential question of whether a man can control his entire life, or whether destiny eventually will take command.

Hemingway's famous concepts about how people should live were frequently expressed in his writing, but in each case these ideas were not really complete. His well-established Code of "Grace Under Pressure" and the necessity of accepting death were never quite adequate because they did not designate any course of action by which one could extend control over life into the control of death.

One of the earliest illustrations of this deficiency in his ideas occurred in the short story "Indian Camp." In this story, Nick Adams accompanied his father on a trip to an Indian village where Dr. Adams planned to help an Indian woman with a difficult childbirth. The woman, who had been in labor for two days, was very distraught and could have died. As Nick became aware of his inability to control the situation, he

1

2

became very uneasy though he didn't take any action. The woman's cries heightened his anxiety about his uselessness until he begged, "Oh, Daddy, can't you give her something to make her stop screaming?" Nick's obvious apprehension over the fact that he could not control this aspect of his life is interesting when one finds that Hemingway did not present any solution to the problem.

In the novel, A Farewell to Arms, Frederic Henry encountered a similar situation. At the end of the book, as Catherine was dying, Frederic realized that destiny had taken control of his life; he could not control whether Catherine lived or died. Confused, upset by this actuality, he argued with himself,

> So now they got her in the end. You never got away with
> anything. Get away hell! It would have been the same if
> we had been married fifty times. And what if she should
> die? She won't die. People don't die in childbirth
> nowadays. That was what all husbands thought. Yes, but
> what if she should die? She won't die. She's just having
> a bad time. The initial labor is usually protracted. She's
> only having a bad time. Afterward we'd say what a bad time
> and Catherine would say it wasn't really so bad. But what
> if she should die? She can't, I tell you. Don't be a fool.
> It's just a bad time. It's just nature giving her hell.
> (Hemingway, 1969, p. 320)

It was at this point that Hemingway began to develop his final plot: A man cannot rely on fate, but he must try to control his life and his death. Frederic's actions immediately became more animated, and he even found some comfort in regulating Catherine's anesthetic. Although he knew that the gas would not actually prolong Catherine's life, it was his first attempt to control death--the beginning of Hemingway's final plot.

Near the end of his life, Hemingway repeated the idea that one should control as much of one's life as possible. In referring to his friend Antonio, who was considering retiring from bullfighting, he felt good that the bullfighter could make his own decision:

3

> No one can advise you on something as delicate as your own
> machinery. But . . . when you're the champ, it's better
> to step down on the best day you've had than to wait until
> it's leaving you and everyone notices. (Hotchner, 1966,
> p. 262)

By retiring, Antonio would be controlling his life, rather than waiting
until something forced him to quit. The author's repetition of this idea
was significant because he would soon face the ultimate test: Could this
control over one's life be applied to one's death, or would fate have the
final control?

The conclusion to Ernest Hemingway's final plot was composed when he
was forced to resolve his own loss of control over his life. The desperation which he felt over this loss was apparent in his conversations with
his friend, A. E. Hotchner. In his biography, Papa Hemingway, Hotchner
referred to his talks with the author, to one of Hemingway's outbursts
that foreshadowed his suicide:

> Hotch, if I can't exist on my own terms, then existence
> is impossible. Do you understand? That is how I've
> lived, and that is how I must live--or not live. (Hotch-
> ner, 1966, p. 328)

Hotchner suggested that Hemingway retire, but this failed to comfort the
despair over his loss of control. Hotchner realized the problem:

> . . . unlike your baseball player and your prize fighter
> and your matador, how does a writer retire? No one ac-
> cepts that his legs are shot or the whiplash gone from his
> reflexes. Everywhere he goes, he hears the same goddamn
> question--What are you working on? (Hotchner, 1966, p.
> 298)

With the belief that he wouldn't be allowed to retire and his personal conviction that he could no longer write, Hemingway felt that his
opportunities for action were quickly diminishing. He felt that his
control over his life was slipping. He then asked,

> What does a man care about? Staying healthy. Working
> good. Eating and drinking with his friends. Enjoying
> himself in bed. I haven't any of them. Do you understand,
> goddamn it? None of them. (Hotchner, 1966, pp. 299-300)

4

Ernest Hemingway no longer possessed the ability to enjoy life. His marked loss of control over what he could and could not do left him very little reason to continue. A broken man who knew it, he refused to forget his personal Code: "a man can be defeated, but not destroyed." He would not resign the ultimate control to destiny, so on July 2, 1961, Ernest Hemingway completed his final plot. By taking his own life, he committed the final act of control. He determined his own death, resolving at last the question which has puzzled him throughout his life: How much of man's life can he control?

Bibliography

Baker, Carlos. Ernest Hemingway. New York: Scribner's, 1969.

Hemingway, Ernest. A Farewell to Arms. New York: Scribner's, 1969.

Hemingway, Mary Welsh. How It Was. New York: Alfred A. Knopf, 1976.

Hotchner, A. E. Papa Hemingway. New York: Random House, 1966.

Instructor's Comments

1. Strengths. This paper uses an interesting technique that can be a useful model to students: a direct quotation beneath the title which triggers the first paragraph as well as the entire position. The writer also was sensitive to two of the writing goals of this assignment--weaving together biography and fiction and experimenting with direct quotations--including footnoting them. And finally, she has a strong profile position from title to final sentence, one that should intrigue her readers since Hemingway's fiction is so auto-biographical.

5

2. <u>Weaknesses</u>. Long quotations, such as the one from <u>A Farewell to Arms</u>, can dilute the impact of a position. More editing and indirect quoting might have been more successful. Perhaps even more biographical documentation of the agonies of Hemingway's final days, such as his long list of physical problems, might have been exploited in describing the "final plot."

PAPER V: PAPER OF CHOICE
DAYS 58–69

DAY 58: CONSIDERING READING CHOICES FOR PAPER V

Goals

1. To suggest topics for Paper V, the paper of choice.
2. To note writing problems special to this paper.

Materials

1. Copies of *The Short Stories of Ernest Hemingway.*
2. Handout 13: Suggestions for Paper V.
3. Handout 14: Student Model for Paper V.

Assignment

1. Ask students to note the DUE date for the fifth paper on the Schedule, Day 69.
2. Remind students that the defenses of Paper IV (the Profile Paper) will begin on Day 63.

Procedure

1. This time students may select any book or long story that has not been studied in class. Assess the time remaining in the semester and consider the interests and reading skills of individual students in suggesting whether a student should read another book or a long story for this assignment. Briefly review the materials, giving plot summaries. Suggestions:

   #### Books

   The Torrents of Spring (1926). A minor work and a parody of Sherwood Anderson.

   Death in the Afternoon (1932). Hemingway's nonfictional study of the art and tragedy of bullfighting.

   Green Hills of Africa (1935). Hunting with Hemingway in Africa.

   To Have and Have Not (1937). In a three-part novel, a Key West fishing boat captain finds adventure smuggling Chinese, Cuban revolutionaries, and bootleg liquor.

   For Whom the Bell Tolls (1940). A major work in which an American goes to the Spanish Civil War to aid the Loyalists in blowing up a bridge and discovers the spirit of humanity.

   Across the River and into the Trees (1950). The critics attacked this novel of a fifty-five-year-old American army colonel who goes to Venice during the last three days of his life.

   A Moveable Feast (1964). A posthumous memoir in which Hemingway remembers Paris, his people, and the 1920s, when life was young.

   Islands in the Stream (1970). Posthumous sea novel.

   #### Stories

   "The Undefeated" (1925). The story of an aging bullfighter who refuses to quit.

   "Fifty Grand" (1927). The story of a champion boxer who bets against himself.

   "The Gambler, the Nun, and the Radio" (1933). The story of people's adjustments to the world as seen by the hospitalized Mr. Frazer.

   "The Snows of Kilimanjaro" (1936). The story of a dying American in Africa who reflects upon death and a misused life.

   "The Short Happy Life of Francis Macomber" (1936). A hunting safari in Africa becomes a drama of Macomber's search for honor and manhood.

2. Distribute and discuss Handout 13: Suggestions for Paper V.
3. Stress that this paper should be especially clear about the basic plot and characters since most readers will not have read the material.
4. You may distribute Handout 14: Student Model for Paper V now or reserve it for discussion later.

DAYS 59–62: READING HEMINGWAY MATERIAL OF CHOICE AND PREPARING FOR DEFENSE DAY

Goals

1. To provide time for students to read the Hemingway material of choice.
2. To prepare for Defense Day on Paper IV.

Materials

1. *The Short Stories of Ernest Hemingway.*
2. Copies of the profile papers chosen for Defense Day.

Procedure

1. Days 59–62 give students time to read the book or story of their choice and the instructor time to correct the profile papers.
2. On Day 62, hand out the profile papers to be used during Defense Day. If you will require more than one Defense Day, decide which students will be responsible for defenses on each day. Do not return the corrected papers until all defenses are complete.

DAYS 63–65: PARTICIPATING IN DEFENSE DAY AND FOLLOW-UP

Goals

1. To allow students to defend the position taken in the Hemingway Profile Paper.
2. To consider autobiographical insights of major Hemingway critics.

Materials

1. Again, extra copies of the papers for defense may be needed.
2. Corrected papers to be returned when the defenses have been completed.

Procedure

1. More than one Defense Day may be necessary if all students are to have defended at least one Position Paper before the seventh paper. The Profile Paper is a likely time for scheduling consecutive days of discussion because it provides interesting new information and builds toward the Summation Paper.
2. Day 65 is follow-up, and you again have the options of discussing the papers of other students, the student model papers (Handouts 11 and 12), or the observations of literary critics. Suggestions for the latter include (1) Malcolm Cowley's profile, "A Portrait of Mister Papa," in *Life* (January 10, 1949), which was revised and appeared in *Ernest Hemingway: The Man and His Work,* edited by John K. M. McCaffery, pp. 34–56; and (2) Philip Young's "The Man and His Legend" in *Ernest Hemingway: A Reconsideration,* pp. 147–52, 170–71.

DAYS 66–69: COMPLETING PAPER V AND LOOKING TOWARD PAPER VI

Goals

1. To provide time to complete the writing, revision, and proofreading of Paper V.
2. To introduce Paper VI.

Procedure

1. Use Days 66–68 for in-class time to write and proofread Paper V, which is due on Day 69.
2. Collect the papers of choice and, as soon as possible, choose those that will be used during Defense Day.

3. Remind students that Paper VI will focus on a short work, one that appeared in an issue of *Life* magazine. Yet, *The Old Man and the Sea* is a major work, one that was instrumental in Hemingway's winning the Nobel Prize. Many students may have already read it or seen the film on television. It is an immensely readable book, a popular short novel that students will like. It is a fish story—and much more.

4. Like all Hemingway novels, *The Old Man and the Sea* has its origins in the author's life, although it is not so autobiographical as some. The story does come from Hemingway's life in Key West, from his love of fishing and the sea, from his years in Cuba. To suggest its early origins, read aloud Hemingway's April 1936 *Esquire* article "On the Blue Water: A Gulf Stream Letter" (see Appendix D).

HANDOUT 13
SUGGESTIONS FOR PAPER V: PAPER OF CHOICE

Books

1. *The Torrents of Spring* (1926)
   a. Carlos Baker sees this parody-satire as Hemingway's first public announcement that he was on his own. Expand on this idea.
   b. What are the hazards of parody such as this? Should Hemingway have written this book?

2. *Death in the Afternoon* (1932)
   a. Why was Hemingway so drawn to the bullfight?
   b. Deal with this book in terms of Hemingway's concept of the Hero—a man of action and an artist.

3. *Green Hills of Africa* (1935)
   a. Expand on Hemingway's affection for Mark Twain's *Huckleberry Finn.*
   b. Hemingway wrote in the introduction that he attempted to write "an absolutely true book." What is truth in this book?

4. *To Have and Have Not* (1937)
   a. Consider Harry Morgan as an American with his roots in American values, a nineteenth-century man destroyed in the twentieth.
   b. Deal with the two parts of the title.

5. *For Whom the Bell Tolls* (1940)
   a. How does this novel differ from previous works?
   b. What is the significance of Maria?
   c. Deal with a symbol, e.g., Donne's sermon *(Devotions XII),* the bridge, the airplanes.

6. *Across the River and into the Trees* (1950)
   a. Review the background of the title and explain its choice for this post-World War II novel.
   b. Analyze wind as symbol in the novel.

7. *A Moveable Feast* (1964)
   a. How does Hemingway treat his fellow writers?
   b. Deal with the title in terms of the total impact of the book.

8. *Islands in the Stream* (1970)
   a. Consider the book in terms of Hemingway's suicide.
   b. This sea novel was written during the same time as *The Old Man and the Sea.* Why didn't Hemingway release it then? Some critics said that it needs revision. Do you agree?

Stories

1. "The Undefeated" (1925)
   a. Can this story be seen as more than a bullfighting story? Does it say something about the young and the old today?
   b. The title seems to relate to the Code. How?

2. "Fifty Grand" (1927)
   a. One critic says that this story is a portrait of an individual who exemplifies the theme of the "adjusted" man. What does that mean?
   b. This is a story of irony. What is the essential irony?

3. "The Gambler, the Nun, and the Radio" (1933)
   a. How do all three parts of the title relate to the theme of the story?
   b. What is the meaning of the setting, the hospital?

4. "The Snows of Kilimanjaro" (1936)
   a. Expand on a symbol, e.g., the leopard, Harry's death by gangrene.
   b. Why would Hemingway say that this story was "about as good as any" of his writings? (See Carlos Baker, *Hemingway: The Writer as Artist,* p. 191)

5. "The Short Happy Life of Francis Macomber" (1936)
   a. Analyze why Macomber's wife shot him.
   b. Examine the title. What does the word "happy" mean?

HANDOUT 14
STUDENT MODEL FOR PAPER V

ONE'S RESPONSIBILITY TO HUMANITY

by Emily Buss

"For what are we living?" This is one of the most serious questions
that plagues our minds throughout our lives. Many believe we ought to
live to serve a god. Others feel we should live merely to gratify our own
selfish wants. In For Whom the Bell Tolls, Ernest Hemingway picks a third
alternative. He writes that each one of us must live for the good of
every human being. His belief in an individual's responsibility to the
whole is expressed in the passage by John Donne from which Hemingway took
his title.

> No man is an Island, intire of it selfe; every man is
> a peace of the Continent, a part of the maine; if a Clod
> bee washed away by the Sea, Europe is the lesse, as well
> as if a Promontorie were, as well as if a Mannor of they
> friens or of thine owne were; any mans death diminishes me,
> because I am involved in Mankinde; And therefore never send
> to know for whom the bell tolls; It tolls for thee.

Hemingway expresses this idea of one's responsibility to Mankind through
several of his characters, particularly the central character, Robert
Jordan.

For Whom the Bell Tolls is the story of a young American professor,
Robert Jordan, who is a dynamiter for the Republicans in the Spanish
Civil War. Jordan is assigned to blow up a bridge held by the Fascists
as a part of a Republican offensive. For three days, he lives behind
enemy lines with the guerilla band which will help him destroy the bridge.
Hemingway's entire novel takes place during these three days. While in

1

2

the mountains, Jordan falls in love with Maria, a young girl once held as
a Fascist prisoner. In addition, Jordan must deal with the cowardice and
mutiny of Pablo, the fallen leader of the peasant band; the strong-minded
and even bitter nature of Pilar, Pablo's wife; and the gradual crumbling
of his support for the attack. At the end of the story, Jordan success-
fully blows up the bridge. Several of the guerilla band are killed, but
Pablo, Pilar, and Maria escape unharmed. Robert Jordan does not go with
them for his badly wounded leg virtually immobilizes him. In his last
moments of life, despite his unbearable pain, Jordan prepares to shoot a
Fascist officer. In the short time he spends in the mountains, Jordan
learns a great deal about life. "I wish there was some way to pass on
what I've learned, though," he said. "Christ, I was learning fast there
at the end" (Hemingway, 1940, p. 467).

Hemingway first expresses his idea that every person is obligated to
a cause greater than himself through Jordan's thoughts about his father
and grandfather. Jordan's grandfather was involved in a great deal of
warfare which required a vast amount of courage. Such courage, Jordan
feels, could only come from a concern for humanity rather than for oneself.
Like his grandfather, Jordan is making great sacrifices and risking his
own life for a cause he believes in: the liberty of the Spanish people.
His father, on the other hand, committed suicide. To Jordan, such an act
seems cowardly and selfish.

> [Jordan] realized that if there was such a thing as [a
> hereafter] both he and his grandfather would be acutely
> embarrassed by the presence of his father. Anyone has a
> right to [commit suicide, he thought]. . . . But it isn't
> a good thing to do. I understand it, but I do not approve
> of it. . . . You have to be awfully occupied with yourself
> to do a thing like that. (Hemingway, 1940, p. 338)

As the time of his attack draws near and his tension mounts, Jordan's
bitterness towards those who avoid war because of selfish fears increases.

3

>   Durriti [a Republican military leader] was good and his
>   own people shot him. . . . Shot him because he wanted them
>   to attack. . . . The cowardly swine. (Hemingway, 1940, p.
>   370)

Robert Jordan feels a similar disgust toward Pablo when Pablo runs away from the camp the night before the offensive. Throughout the story Pablo shows a great dislike for Jordan and his mission, for he realizes the destruction of the bridge will force his gang from the security of their mountain home. Already a coward, Pablo loathes Robert Jordan who brings great danger to his band. As the attack on the bridge becomes imminent, Pablo perceives the virtual impossibility of Jordan's mission. In a selfish attempt to protect himself and ruin the mission he detests, Pablo sneaks from the camp with some of Jordan's equipment. This self-centered act throws Jordan into a rage.

>   Muck the whole treachery ridden country. Muck their
>   [the Spanish leaders'] egotism and their selfishness and
>   their egotism and their conceit and their treachery. . . .
>   God muck Pablo. Pablo is all of them. (Hemingway, 1940,
>   pp. 369-370)

The morning following Pablo's mutiny, he returns. He returns because he, too, is learning that each man owes his life service to mankind. Pablo realizes it is not enough to follow one's selfish desires, and upon his return he confesses to Pilar, "Having done such a thing [deserting his fellow men] there is a loneliness that cannot be borne" (Hemingway, 1940, p. 390).

Hemingway's belief that each individual must contribute to a larger community is revealed to a lesser extent by other characters. Andres, a member of Pablo's gang whom Jordan sends with an emergency message to Republican headquarters, realizes that all he possesses only has worth if it is given away. Reflecting sadly on his life, Andres discovers he is worthless to himself.

4

> You have four grenades in your pocket, but they are only
> good to throw away. You have a carbine on your back but it
> is only good to give away bullets. You have a message to
> give away. . . . Everything you have is to give. (Hemingway,
> 1940, p. 368)

Like Robert Jordan, Maria expresses a desire to forget her selfish inter-

ests and take her place in the group. As the gang prepares to leave the

mountains towards the end of the novel, Maria refuses to take a safer

position in the line of retreating horses as Jordan tells her to. "'Nay,'

she told him. . . . 'I go in the order that I am to go'" (Hemingway, 1940,

p. 458).

The best expression of Hemingway's belief that one must cast aside

selfish ideas to serve mankind is found in the last pages of For Whom the

Bell Tolls, when Robert Jordan realizes he is about to die. Jordan is

left alone with a badly fractured femur, not far from the enemy which is

unable to advance because of the destroyed bridge. Fully aware that his

death is near, he thinks not of himself, but of the cause and the people

to whom he has devoted his life.

> I [Jordan] hate to leave [life] very much and I hope
> I have done some good in it. I have tried to with what
> talent I had. (Hemingway, 1940, p. 467)

In his last moments of life, he is still able to struggle for the freedom

of the Spanish people. As the enemy begins to detour around the useless

bridge, it enters Jordan's firing range. He wants above all things to be

useful up to the last minutes of his life. "You better get fixed around

some way where you will be useful instead of leaning against this tree

like a tramp," he thinks. (466) However, the pain caused by Jordan's leg

wound is almost unbearable, and he is continuously tempted to kill himself

to escape his agony. As his life draws to a close, Jordan refuses to

gratify his selfish wants as long as he is still able to serve the

Spanish people.

5

> No, it isn't [all right to kill yourself]. Because
> there is something you can do yet. . . . If you wait and
> hold [the enemy] even a little while or just get the
> officer that may make all the difference. (Hemingway,
> 1940, p. 470)

It would be unfair not to mention that Hemingway later committed suicide. This suicide clearly does not coincide with the ideas he expressed in his novel, For Whom the Bell Tolls. In considering this point one must realize that Ernest Hemingway probably was attempting to describe an ideal human trait which he wished to attain, not a trait that he believed he had already attained. Through the attitudes of his characters, Hemingway reveals his own ideas on how our lives should be lived. In For Whom the Bell Tolls, he tells us to live for one another and not for ourselves.

Bibliography

Hemingway, Ernest.   For Whom the Bell Tolls.   New York: Scribner's, 1940.

Instructor's Comments

1. Strengths. This paper is especially successful in the clear description of plot and character, a major goal of the assignment since many students may not have read the novel. Her logical focus on Robert Jordan, her organization of the supporting characters, her use of concrete detail--all those document her title and her position.

2. Weaknesses. The conclusion raises issues that might best be left alone. While Hemingway's suicide is an interesting aside, the writer might have been more successful in keeping her reader on target by either referring to material read earlier by the seminar or by restatement.

PAPER VI: "THE OLD MAN AND THE SEA" DAYS 70–79

DAYS 70–71: READING "THE OLD MAN AND THE SEA"

Goal

To provide class time to read *The Old Man and the Sea* (1952).

Materials

Copies of *The Old Man and the Sea* or *Three Novels: The Sun Also Rises, A Farewell to Arms, The Old Man and the Sea.*

Assignment

Ask students to note on the Schedule the DUE date of Paper VI, Day 79.

Procedure

1. Begin by reviewing briefly the earlier discussion of the *Esquire* article "On the Blue Water."
2. Remind students that *The Old Man and the Sea*, first published in *Life* magazine, won the 1953 Pulitzer Prize and was instrumental in Hemingway's winning the 1954 Nobel Prize. More will be said about this on Day 72.
3. Ask students to note the dedication: "To Charlie Scribner and to Max Perkins." Scribner, of course, was Hemingway's longtime friend and publisher. Maxwell Perkins was Hemingway's Scribner editor and friend, one of the most famous editors in American literature; he was especially noted for his work with Thomas Wolfe.
4. Most students will be able to complete the novel during these two days.

Additional Suggestion

If the budget allows, order the 1958 Warner Brothers production of *The Old Man and the Sea* starring Spencer Tracy as Santiago. The film is especially interesting since Hemingway watched the filmmaking and later called it a waste of time.

DAY 72: DISCUSSING HEMINGWAY AND THE NOBEL AND PULITZER PRIZES

Goal

To provide background information on Hemingway's winning of the Nobel and Pulitzer Prizes.

Materials

1. Texts of the Nobel Prize Citation and Nobel Prize Speech (included at the end of the outline for Day 72).
2. You may wish to use two references: (a) W. J. Stuckey's *The Pulitzer Prize Novels*, pp. 165–70; (b) *American Winners of the Nobel Literary Prize*, edited by Warren G. French and Walter E. Kidd, specifically the chapter "Ernest Hemingway" by Ken Moritz, pp. 158–92.

Procedure

1. After the criticism of his 1950 novel *Across the River and into the Trees*, Hemingway wrote *The Old Man and the Sea*, which restored his reputation. The 1952 novel had been brewing for a long time. (Here you might wish to read chapter 4, "The Boy and the Sea," in *Hemingway and Jake* by Vernon

"Jake" Klimo and Will Oursler, pp. 35–38.)
The novel won Hemingway the 1953 Pulitzer
Prize and was instrumental in his being
chosen in 1954 as the sixth American writer
ever to win the Nobel Prize.

2. At this point, review the two prizes.

   a. *The Pulitzer Prize.* When Joseph Pulitzer
died in 1911, he left a fortune of nearly
$19 million amassed through his develop-
ment of sensational journalism; owner of
the St. Louis *Post-Dispatch* and the New
York *World,* he nevertheless felt his work
to have integrity. So in 1903 he convinced Columbia University to enhance
the field of journalism by establishing a
school of journalism—and he gave $1
million for the project. Then, he was
persuaded to use half of another million-
dollar gift for his pet project: annual
cash prizes for journalism and letters.
Thus the Pulitzer Prizes were established.
An advisory board was placed in charge
of the $1000 prizes, including the cate-
gory of the best novel: "Annually, for
the American novel published during the
year which shall best present the wholesome atmosphere of American life and
the highest standard of American man-
ners and manhood, $1000" (Stuckey,
The Pulitzer Prize Novels, p. 6). The
prizes for novels began in 1917.

      Through the years, the advisory board
wrestled with the problem of the standards for choosing a winner, especially
the problem of "wholesome" since many
famous novels, such as *The Sun Also
Rises,* challenged American life. The
wording was changed and expanded,
though the concern for "moral" standards led to rejection of Hemingway's
early novels: physical love outside marriage in *A Farewell to Arms* disturbed
the judges; the rather explicit sex of *For
Whom the Bell Tolls* was distasteful to
the honorary chairman of the advisory
board, though the other members voted
for the novel. But in 1953 *The Old Man
and the Sea* was found to be sufficiently
wholesome to pass the test.

   b. *The Nobel Prize.* The Nobel Prize for
Literature was one of five international
awards established in the 1895 will of
Swedish industrialist Alfred Nobel, the
inventor of dynamite. The prize "to
the person who shall have produced in
the field of Literature the most distin-
guished work of an idealistic tendency"
(French and Kidd, eds., *American Winners of the Nobel Literary Prize,* p. 6) is
directed by the Nobel Foundation; the
annual award includes a large cash gift
(from the accrued interest of Nobel's
original gift), a gold medal, and a diplo-
ma bearing the winner's name and field
of achievement. Like the Pulitzer Board,
the Nobel judges may decide not to give
an award for a particular year.

      The first awards were given in 1901,
but no American writer received one
until 1930. Hemingway became the sixth
winner on the American list, which has
since increased to nine: Sinclair Lewis,
1930; Eugene O'Neill, 1936; Pearl Buck,
1938; T. S. Eliot (then a British citizen),
1948; William Faulkner, 1949; Hemingway, 1954; John Steinbeck, 1962; Saul
Bellow, 1976; Isaac Bashevis Singer,
1978.

3. Present the texts of the Nobel Prize Citation
and Nobel Prize Speech (see below). Play
again the Caedmon record/tape, *Ernest Hemingway Reading,* that includes Hemingway
reading his Nobel Address.

4. Background stories on Hemingway's Nobel
Prize may have been covered during Anecdote Day; nevertheless, review is advisable.
See Carlos Baker's *Ernest Hemingway: A
Life Story,* "The Bounty of Sweden," pp.
525–29. Hemingway was unable to make
the trip to Stockholm for the award largely
because the fifty-five-year-old author was on
the mend from an airplane crash in Uganda.
He had suffered a ruptured kidney, a cracked
skull, two compressed and one cracked verte-
bra, and serious burns.

5. It is interesting to discuss awards at this
point, since many writers both want them
and fear them. Fame, recognition, sudden
popularity can be time-consuming, distract-
ing from one's work, the kiss of death.
Writers like John Steinbeck believed that
little good material was written by Nobel

winners after they received their awards. Some writers were even driven to suicide after winning the Pulitzer (see Leggett, *Ross and Tom: Two American Tragedies*). The period might conclude with a discussion: Why does a writer write? Why did Hemingway write?

Nobel Prize Citation

Hemingway's Nobel Citation reads as follows:

For his powerful, style-forming mastery of the art of modern narration, as most recently evinced in *The Old Man and the Sea.*

Swedish Academy

At the December 10 ceremony, Anders Oesterling, permanent secretary of the Swedish Academy, expanded upon the citation:

. . . Hemingway's earlier writings display brutal, cynical and callous signs which may be considered at variance with the Nobel Prize requirements for a work of ideal tendencies. But on the other hand, he also possesses a heroic pathos which forms the basic element of his awareness of life, a manly love of danger and adventure, with a natural admiration of every individual who fights the good fight in a world of reality overshadowed by violence and death. . . . [The central theme of courage can be seen in] the bearing of one who is put to the test and who steels himself to meet the cold cruelty of existence without by so doing repudiating the great and generous moments. . . . [He is] one of the great writers of our time, one of those who, honestly and undauntedly, reproduces the genuine features of the hard countenance of the age. . . . [French and Kidd, eds., *American Winners*, pp. 158–59.]

The Nobel Prize Speech

In 1954 Ernest Hemingway was awarded the Nobel Prize for Literature, an award that carried a $35,000 check, a gold medal (which he later presented to the Virgin of Cobre, Cuba's national saint, and kept in the shrine of Our Lady at Santiago de Cuba), and the opportunity to make a speech in Stockholm. Since he felt that giving the speech would interrupt his work, invade his privacy, and produce distasteful publicity—and because he was still recuperating from his African airplane crashes—he sent along a speech with the American Ambassador to Sweden, John Cabot, who accepted the prize on Hemingway's behalf:

Members of the Swedish Academy, Ladies and Gentlemen: Having no facility for speechmaking nor any domination of rhetoric, I wish to thank the administrators of the generosity of Alfred Nobel for this prize. No writer who knows the great writers who did not receive the prize can accept it other than with humility. There is no need to list these writers. Everyone here may make his own list according to his knowledge and his conscience. It would be impossible for me to ask the Ambassador of my country to read a speech in which a writer said all of the things which are in his heart. Things may not be immediately discernible in what a man writes, and in this sometimes he is fortunate; but eventually they are quite clear and by these and the degree of alchemy that he possesses he will endure or be forgotten. Writing, at its best, is a lonely life. Organizations for writers palliate the writer's loneliness but I doubt if they improve his writing. He grows in public stature as he sheds his loneliness and often his work deteriorates. For he does his work alone and if he is a good writer he must face eternity, or the lack of it, each day. For a true writer each book should be a new beginning where he tries again for something that is beyond attainment. He should always try for something that has never been done or that others have tried and failed. Then sometimes, with great luck, he will succeed. How simple the writing of literature would be if it were only necessary to write in another way what has been well written. It is because we have had such great writers in the past that a writer is driven far out past where he can go, out to where no one can help him. I have spoken too long for a writer. A writer should write what he has to say and not speak it. Again I thank you. [Horst Frenz, ed., *Nobel Lectures: Literature, 1901–1967*, pp. 501–2.]

DAYS 73–76: CHOOSING A TOPIC FOR PAPER VI AND PARTICIPATING IN DEFENSE DAY AND FOLLOW-UP

Goals

1. To suggest topics for Paper VI.
2. To complete the Defense Day and follow-up discussion of the Papers of Choice.

Materials

1. Handout 15: Suggestions for Paper VI.
2. Handout 16: Student Model for Paper VI.
3. Copies of papers for Defense Day on Paper V.
4. Corrected papers to distribute at the end of Defense Day.

Procedure

1. Distribute Handout 15 on Day 73 and discuss positions for papers on *The Old Man and the Sea.* Handout 16 may also be discussed at this time.
2. Distribute the papers to be considered on Defense Day on Day 74. The day may be given over to studying these papers or to beginning the drafts of Paper VI.
3. Defense Day is held on Day 75, following the procedure outlined in the introduction, The Seminar Method. Return all corrected papers at the end of the hour.
4. For the follow-up discussion on Day 76, you may use the papers of other students, the Student Model (Handout 16), or the discussion of a critic such as Richard Hovey's essay "*The Snows of Kilimanjaro:* The Triumph of Death," in *Hemingway: The Inward Terrain*, pp. 127–31.

DAYS 77–79: COMPLETING PAPER VI AND LOOKING TOWARD THE FINAL PAPER

Goals

1. To provide time to complete Paper VI.
2. To orient students to the final paper.

Procedure

1. Days 77 and 78 should be given over to writing and proofreading Paper VI.

2. On Day 79, collect the papers. As soon as possible, select and reproduce the papers to be used in the final Defense Day discussions.
3. Orient students to the final paper by suggesting that it offers a number of alternatives:
   a. If time allows, you may wish to assign two papers—a serious summation of Ernest Hemingway and his work and a parody assignment.
   b. If time is short and spirits weary, you may wish to be more flexible. Students may elect to write either a serious or a humorous paper. Even the length may be shortened to three pages.
   c. Another possibility that has worked very well: agree to give a grade of A to any final paper that is read aloud to the seminar. These presentations may take two or three days, but they release final tensions. There is, then, no Defense Day for Paper VII; instead, there is a chance for creativity and an opportunity to summarize. In addition, everyone is justifiably rewarded for having cooperated throughout the course. Note: still require that Paper VII be typed.
4. Refer to Handout 2: The Hemingway Chronology for a last time, noting Hemingway's death and the posthumous publications. You may also wish to refer to Hemingway's funeral. An interesting account is found in Leicester Hemingway, *My Brother*, pp. 11–13.

HANDOUT 15
SUGGESTIONS FOR PAPER VI: "THE OLD MAN AND THE SEA" (1952)

1. Why was this novel so important in Hemingway's winning the Nobel Prize?
2. Is the Old Man just an old man or does he represent something else? Try to define him as a symbol.
3. What is the function of the boy Manolin?
4. Some see this novel as a parable. Review the meaning of "parable" and try to define your position in this way.
5. Take a key line, such as the last one in the book, and try to mold your position around that line.
6. Joe DiMaggio is mentioned in the novel more than once. Could this lead to a position?
7. This novel also won the Pulitzer Prize. Do some research on the prize and the historical period. Why do you think the book won the award during the Cold War?
8. Contrast or compare this novel with another story, such as "The Big Two-Hearted River" or the *Esquire* article "On the Blue Water."
9. Explain how this later work is an *extension* of earlier Nick Adams stories, such as "The Big Two-Hearted River."
10. Is Santiago a Code Hero? Can he be contrasted with another Hemingway character?
11. Does this novel suggest a religious comparison? Is it a Christian story?
12. Can this novel be seen in terms of biography, of an aging and wounded author beset by adversity, by critics?
13. One critic said that the book is related to the "American Dream." Can you accept this? What does this mean?
14. Examine the style. Does it relate to the theme?
15. Consider the ending. Is this story tragic or basically triumphant?

HANDOUT 16
STUDENT MODEL FOR PAPER VI

DETERMINATION AND FAITH

by Anne Nusser

In Ernest Hemingway's 1952 novel, The Old Man and the Sea, self-determination and faith were the two forces which drove the old fisherman Santiago to be an achiever. He was an achiever in the sense that his goals were personal rather than materialistic. His success was in believing in himself and having the strength to hold up his head and be proud of himself even when society labeled him as a "failure" and "defeated." This strong belief was one which he carried with him and used to help him survive.

Hemingway first suggests this belief in self-determination in his description of Santiago. He described the old man as having skin which was blotched from many years of fishing in the sun: "His hands had deep-creased scars from handling heavy fish on the cords. But none of these scars were fresh. They were as old as erosions in a fishless desert." This description reveals a man who had lived a hard life. The scars showed the many hardships that he had gone through and that he had been able to survive these hard times. The words "fishless desert" emphasized the fact that Santiago had been labeled a "failure" by other fishermen. Even though his body appeared defeated, his spirit was not. It was his eyes which showed his inner self. They were "cheerful and undefeated." This was the true spirit by which the old man lived.

1

2

Santiago was an old fisherman who had an unlucky streak in fishing. It had been eighty-four days since he had his last catch. Everyone in the village except the boy Manolin believed that he was an unlucky person; they thought of him as an outcast. Despite this public opinion, he was never defeated. He believed that he would catch fish again. This is stated early in the book when he and Manolin were talking about the lack of faith that Manolin's father had in the old man.

> "He hasn't much faith."
> "No," the old man said. "But we have. Haven't we?"

This reaffirmation of faith only showed this man's determination. He would wait any length of time to again catch fish.

It was when Santiago was struggling with the marlin that he again showed his determination and courage. While fighting, he encountered several problems which would have defeated most fishermen, but he held strong so that he could remain victorious. After the fish had dragged him out to sea, his back, which was anchoring the lines, became stiff and sore. To try and counteract this feeling, Santiago talked himself into feeling comfortable. He wanted to catch this fish, and he was not willing to let his body be a factor against him.

After his back pains, his right hand became cut by the line when the fish lurched forward. He was not happy that his hand was hurt so early in the struggle. However, he did not let it bother him because he did not want to give the marlin any clues that he had been injured. A short time later, his left hand became cramped. He tried to massage it to get it to open, but it would not relax. He decided to leave it alone and let the sun's warmth heal it. Santiago knew that this hand had been through much abuse and that was why it had become cramped. He also felt sure that if he needed it in an emergency he could open it: "I will open it, cost whatever it costs." With two injured hands many men would have given up.

3

But with all of the old man's determination, he knew that he could count on his inner strength to help him heal his hands if they were needed in a crisis.

Struggling with the fish caused Santiago to become fatigued. He knew he had to sleep, but through the art of positive thinking he convinced his body that it was not necessary. He received his strength from thoughts. The first was about his hero, Joe DiMaggio. He knew that in baseball this man had both youth and strength on his side. That is what Santiago needed now, and he drew those two strengths into his body by thinking about them. The other thought was of his youth. He had arm-wrestled a Black man for one day, and finally he drew up all his strength and smashed his opponent's arm to the table. For this he received the title "El Champéon." He enjoyed this feeling; he wanted to be triumphant again. He knew that he could have the title again if he caught this fish. This gave him more incentive to battle his fatigue. The relief he received was only temporary. Finally, it came to the point where he knew that he must sleep a little. He went to sleep and dreamt about the qualities that he would need to beat the fish. He dreamt of strength, youth, and happiness. Through these dreams, he was able to fill his psychological reservoir which had been emptied. When he awoke, he again was ready to fight the fish.

The marlin finally tired, and Santiago was able to kill him. The struggle consisted of gains and losses on both sides. However, it was the old man who was triumphant over the fish. Santiago now was faced with the return trip home. Even though he had just overcome one struggle, he knew there would be others. This next battle was with the sharks. At first, just a few came and he was able to kill them, but he knew that soon they would come in packs. The sharks would try to defeat him. To this he said, "I am still an old man. But I am not unarmed." With incredible

4

determination, Santiago fought the sharks all night. The sharks, however,
were the victors.

When he arrived on shore at last, he went to his shack to sleep. And
when he awoke, he saw the boy Manolin. Then he and Manolin discussed what
had happened.

> "They beat me, Manolin," he said. "They truly beat me."
> "He didn't beat you. Not the fish."
> "No. Truly. It was afterwards."

Although Santiago seemed to feel defeated at first, he realized that he had
won two victories. The first was over the fish, and the other was for
himself. He knew that he had fought well to win the fish, and he proved
to himself that he still had the strength to do it. This gave him new
courage to try again. He was so determined that he and Manolin began to
make plans to fish again when the old man had rested.

Santiago had many things going against him from the start. He was
old, his body was not that strong anymore, and few people had faith in him.
Although he did not have the physical attributes to prove to the village
that he was not a failure, he had his self-determination and faith to prove
to the people that he was not defeated. This belief in himself helped him
survive. Eventually, it helped him prove to the village that he was
successful.

Instructor's Comments

1. Strengths. This paper reveals a strong outline, keen observation to
   develop each paragraph, and a language which matches the personality
   and emotion of Santiago. It builds convincingly toward its logical
   conclusion. It is a sound position since it defines the triumphant
   quality of the novel. Her use of repetitions, key words, compound

5

sentences with semicolons to tighten the line are all interesting

aspects in terms of the writing goal for Paper VI--to try new writing

techniques.

2. <u>Weaknesses</u>. There is some trouble with position words--"determination,"

"self-determination," "faith," "courage." Perhaps a sharper title

could have come from Hemingway's own words in the novel. Then, too,

even more use of direct quotation would strengthen the position of the

paper and reflect the tone of the novel.

PAPER VII: THE SUMMING UP
DAYS 80–90

DAYS 80–82: BEGINNING THE FINAL PAPER AND PREPARING FOR DEFENSE DAY

Goals

1. To help students select a topic for Paper VII.
2. To provide in-class time to begin writing the final paper.
3. To prepare for Defense Day.

Materials

1. Handout 17: Suggestions for Paper VII, Summing Up.
2. Handout 18: Suggestions for Paper VII, Parody.
3. Handouts 19 and 20: Student Models for Paper VII.
4. Copies of Paper VI (*The Old Man and the Sea*) to be used on Day 82, Defense Day.

Assignment

Ask students to insert the DUE date for Paper VII on the Schedule.

Procedure

1. Define the writing assignment, using Handouts 17 and 18 as a point of departure. Encourage students to review materials in the class library and to re-read their previous papers in preparation for Paper VII. If time allows, you may wish to assign both a summation paper and a humorous paper.
2. The model papers may be distributed and discussed on Day 80 or 81. The remainder of the time should be given over to in-class writing.
3. Hand out on Day 82 copies of the papers to be defended. Students may study these papers in class or continue to work on Paper VII.

DAYS 83–84: PARTICIPATING IN DEFENSE DAY AND FOLLOW-UP

Goal

To complete the Defense Day and follow-up discussion.

Materials

Extra copies of the final position papers for students who have forgotten them.

Procedure

1. Follow the established procedures for Defense Day. Return all papers at the end of the period on Day 83.
2. The final follow-up (Day 84) can be spent discussing other papers, the student models, or the insights of a well-known critic such as Carlos Baker in "The Boy and the Lions," *20th Century Interpretations of "The Old Man and the Sea,"* edited by Katherine T. Jobes, pp. 27–33.

DAYS 85–87: COMPLETING THE FINAL PAPER AND SHARING IT IN CLASS

Goals

1. To provide in-class time to complete Paper VII.
2. To encourage students to share their final paper with the class and to respond to the papers of fellow students.
3. To offer a final scholarly evaluation of Hemingway.

Procedure

1. Day 85 should be given over to the completion of Paper VII.
2. Days 86–87 can be set aside for all students to read aloud their final papers. If you elect to cut off the final pressure by granting a uniform grade of A on Paper VII, the experience will be even more enjoyable, and more students may elect a humorous approach. Although these readings do not constitute a Defense Day, the class should attempt to respond to each paper—and so should the instructor.

Additional Suggestion

You may wish to read a final critical evaluation of Ernest Hemingway. Suggestions: "The Art of Evasion" by Leon Edel (pp. 169–71) or "Hemingway: A Defense" by Philip Young (pp. 171–73) in *Hemingway: A Collection of Critical Essays,* edited by Robert P. Weeks.

DAYS 88–89: ENDING THE SEMINAR WITH A SMILE

Goals

1. To share "take-offs" on Hemingway.
2. To end the seminar in high spirits.

Materials

1. "For Whom the Gong Sounds" by Cornelia Otis Skinner in *American Literature in Parody,* edited by R. P. Falk, pp. 241–44.
2. "The Kilimanjaro Device" by Ray Bradbury in *I Sing the Body Electric,* pp. 3–14.

Procedure

1. The class will enjoy hearing either or both of the parodies listed above (Day 88).
2. On Day 89 you may wish to ask seminar members to give their final impressions of the course, what they feel they have learned; or the class may elect to have a kind of fun day, such as a Twenty-Questions Day or a Charades Day based on Hemingway plots and characters. One of my seminars even planned a Hemingway party, and each student dressed as a character from one of the stories or novels. Some instructors may wish to use this day for a final examination.

DAY 90: EVALUATING THE SEMINAR

Goals

1. To encourage students to evaluate the seminar.
2. To share your own evaluation of the course with students.

Materials

Handout 21: Seminar Evaluation.

Procedure

1. Without comment, ask the students to complete the evaluation anonymously. Collect the evaluations.
2. You may wish to offer some final summary comments and personal reactions to the course. Comments on grades may be in order.

HANDOUT 17
SUGGESTIONS FOR PAPER VII: SUMMING UP

1. Did Hemingway deserve the Nobel Prize?
2. Were his works consistent in theme, in character, in style? Does his writing have a Code? Characterize Ernest Hemingway's world.
3. How did Hemingway treat nature?
4. Was Hemingway an American writer, even though most of his works are not set in America?
5. How does Hemingway treat women in his writing?
6. Is he a classic writer, one that is not bound to topical material, one that will survive in the next hundred years?
7. Which work was your favorite?
8. Develop a theory about Hemingway's style. What was his basic style?
9. While Ernest Hemingway was obviously not religious in the conventional meaning of the word (attending church, an active church member), was he "religious"?
10. Was Hemingway a poetic novelist?
11. Consider his titles. Can you develop a theory about his choices?
12. Some critics feel that Hemingway has little, if anything, to say—few ideas. Do you agree?
13. Examine his Nobel Acceptance Speech. Can this lead to a position?
14. Did Ernest Hemingway have a "death wish"?
15. What is the meaning of "love" in his writings?

HANDOUT 18
SUGGESTIONS FOR PAPER VII: PARODY

1. Try a parody of a work by Hemingway. Take a short story or passage from a novel and distort the famous Hemingway style.

2. Try a parody of Hemingway by taking a simple plot and writing it in the famous Hemingway style. For example, take a children's story such as "Little Red Riding Hood."

3. Write a "recently discovered" work of Ernest Hemingway.

4. Write an imaginary interview with Hemingway.

5. Develop a series of letters between Hemingway and a member of this class.

6. Write a newspaper article about a professor who has found an astounding piece of information that reveals a new side of Hemingway (for example, he really hated to fish).

7. Develop an overblown Hollywood film (much like the film version of "The Killers") about a Nick Adams story, including a cast of contemporary actors from film or TV.

8. Write the first draft of Hemingway's Nobel Prize address which he threw away because Mary didn't like it.

9. Write a personal essay on the agonies this class experienced while studying Ernest Hemingway.

10. Write a personal essay on "Ten Steps to the Understanding and Enjoyment of Ernest Hemingway"—a kind of Robert Benchley approach.

HANDOUT 19
STUDENT MODEL FOR PAPER VII: SUMMING UP

HEMINGWAY: A SENSITIVITY TO LIFE

by Greg Pope

Ernest Hemingway was known as a tough, masculine, crisp, objective writer. He was all of these, yet he was more. Hemingway was a writer of great sensitivity. He was deeply moved by the things he saw in life, more so than most people. Life touched his sensitive mind, and he, in turn, portrayed what he felt.

Considering his background, one is not surprised that Hemingway had a sensitive mind. His mother, Grace, was a highly cultured woman who early taught him to appreciate the fine arts:

> She wanted her children to enjoy life. To her this meant
> above all an awareness of the arts. She saw from the first
> that they all had music lessons. As soon as they were old
> enough, she bought them tickets for symphony concerts,
> operatic performances, and the better plays that came to
> Chicago, and they were encouraged quite early to acquaint
> themselves with the paintings and drawings at the Chicago
> Art Institute. Her own deep-dyed belief in creativity made
> her long to develop the talents of her children to the high-
> est possible level. (Baker, 1969, p. 9)

Ernest's father also contributed to his young son's perceptive awareness of the world. Dr. Hemingway took his family on trips to sylvan northern Michigan where Ernest developed a love for nature that is evident in his writing. His initiation into the darker side of life during this time deeply affected him, a boy with a sensitive mind.

As Ernest grew into manhood, he became a writer with a crisp, fresh style that conveyed the sense impressions of a sensitive mind; his words, as Ford Madox Ford exclaimed, "strike you, each one, as if they were

1

2

pebbles fetched fresh from a brook" (Hemingway, 1953, p. xiv). This was

a writer who perused the paintings of Cezanne and saw in watercolor what

he was attempting to paint in words.

What were the things in life that touched his delicate mind, that

this mind put into words?

First, a profound sensitivity to nature pervades Hemingway's work.

His description of a noble, grand nature is moving:

> We passed through a town and stopped in front of the posada
> and the driver took on several packages. Then we started
> on again, and outside the town the road commenced to mount.
> We were going through farming country with rocky hills that
> sloped down into the fields. The grain-fields went up the
> hillsides. Now as we went higher there was a wind blowing
> the grain. The road was white and dusty, and the dust rose
> under the wheels and hung in the air behind us. The road
> climbed up into the hills and left the rich grain-fields
> below. Now there were only patches of grain on the bare
> hillsides and on each side of the watercourses. . . . Up
> there the country was quite barren and the hills were rocky
> and hard-baked clay furrowed by the rain. (Hemingway, 1926,
> p. 105)

These lines from The Sun Also Rises make the eternal earth the hero of the

novel. In another Hemingway novel, A Farewell to Arms, there is also

beautiful description of nature and weather which form an important total

effect. In virtually all his works, Hemingway describes man in terms of

nature, sometimes struggling violently against its powerful forces. In

his last major work, The Old Man and the Sea, he writes clearly of man and

nature, together and yet in conflict. Santiago and the marlin are

"brothers," yet one must die. The beautiful description is there:

> The clouds over the land now rose like mountains and the
> coast was only a long green line with the gray blue hills
> behind it. The water was a dark blue now, so dark that it
> was almost purple. As he looked down into it he saw the
> red sifting of the plankton in the dark water and the
> strange light they made now . . . nothing showed on the
> surface of the water but some patches of yellow, sun-
> bleached Sargasso weed and the purple, formalized, iri-
> descent, gelatinous bladder of a Portuguese man-of-war
> floating close beside the boat. It turned on its side

3

and then righted itself. It floated cheerfully as a bubble
with its long deadly purple filaments trailing a yard behind
in the water. (Hemingway, 1952, p. 35)

Of course, Hemingway was concerned with man as well as with nature.
Not surprisingly, his sensitive mind saw and portrayed suffering as a
major component of the human condition. There is physical suffering in
his work. The childbirth pains of the woman in "Indian Camp" are an
example from his early work. A Farewell to Arms is dominated by the
suffering of men in war, of Frederic Henry who receives a terrible leg
wound, of women like Catherine Barkley who dies painfully in childbirth.
In The Old Man and the Sea, Santiago undergoes physical torture, an agony
that Hemingway compares to a crucifixion.

Psychological suffering can be even more painful than physical suffering. Hemingway's work is permeated with the suffering of mind as well as
body. In "Indian Camp," the psyche of young, innocent Nick Adams is
shocked by the brutal events he witnesses. The Sun Also Rises is a novel
of people wounded psychologically by World War I, people who lead hedon-
istic lives to cover their deep melancholia. Especially poignant is the
suffering of Jake Barnes and Brett Ashley, who live lives dominated by
frustrated love. Frederic Henry of A Farewell to Arms is nearly crushed
by the strain of war and the death of Catherine; Santiago calls upon all
his mental strength to conquer the marlin.

Perhaps Hemingway's fictional world was so filled with suffering
because his own life was one of pain. Literary biographer Philip Young
chronicles Ernest's wounds:

> His skull was fractured at least once; he sustained at
> least a dozen brain concussions . . . he was in three bad
> automobile accidents . . . in the African jungle he was
> in two airplane accidents in the space of two days, during
> which time he suffered severe internal injuries. . . . In
> warfare he was shot through nine parts of the body. . . .
> (Young, 1965, pp. 25-26)

4

Hemingway saw man in an adverse world, replete with suffering, one in which man could not win.

But through this world of agony, Hemingway did find some redeeming factors in life. Man can be great in the way he reacts to a world of suffering. If a man has courage and endurance, then he is noble and dignified. The life of Jake Barnes in The Sun Also Rises is a frustrated, circular one, but he refuses to wallow in self-pity. Similarly, Frederic Henry has virtually everything he values taken away from him, but he does not crack. But it is in The Old Man and the Sea that Hemingway's view of man's nobility is best developed. Santiago, in his pursuit of the marlin and his defeat by the sharks, remains unbeaten, strong in a world of suffering. He acts in accordance with his maxims: "a man can be destroyed, but not beaten" and "a man is not made for defeat." Santiago is the epitome of man's tragic heroism.

In addition, Hemingway's highly developed aesthetic sense saw man's relationships with fellow human beings as beautiful and delicate. At times during "Indian Camp" Dr. Adams is insensitive to his son Nick, but at the end of the story, as Dr. Adams rows Nick across the lake, there also is a strong and trusting bond between father and son. In The Sun Also Rises, Jake Barnes and Bill Gorton enjoy a deep, personal relationship. In A Farewell to Arms, Rinaldi and Henry, Catherine and Henry, share mutual ties of great warmth and love; these relationships are among the few positive aspects of life in the novel. In The Old Man and the Sea, Santiago and the boy Manolin are two human beings very close to each other. Yes, the world is a tough place, but human love and interdependence soften the blow.

Thus, Hemingway was a man and writer of refined and delicate sensibilities under a tough outer veneer. He was shocked by the terrible

5

violence and suffering in the world. (Perhaps it was so shocking to him that he was fascinated by it, "the fascination with the abomination.") His sensitive mind saw the beautiful and the noble in life as well as the brutality and the agony. He was touched by the beauty and dignity of nature. He was impressed by man's potential of courage in an adverse universe. He saw warm human relationships as desirable. Ernest Hemingway was a sensitive man who lived in the Twentieth Century and portrayed life as he saw it, uncompromisingly.

Bibliography

Baker, Carlos. Ernest Hemingway: A Life Story. New York: Scribner's, 1969.

Hemingway, Ernest. The Old Man and the Sea. New York: Scribner's, 1952.

Hemingway, Ernest. The Sun Also Rises. New York: Scribner's, 1926.

Hemingway, Ernest. The Hemingway Reader. Edited by Charles Poore. New York: Scribner's, 1953.

Young, Philip. Ernest Hemingway. Rev. ed. Minneapolis: University of Minnesota Press, 1965.

Instructor's Comments

This summation paper is a lesson in synthesis. Appreciative, it weaves biography, research, the common seminar readings, sharp (if rather lengthy) direct quotations, and personal reflection together. The writer remembers—words, themes, characters. He reveals the total experience of the course, his sensitivity to literature, to the man and writer Ernest Hemingway. His title, his introduction, his paragraphs and prose and punctuation, his conclusion are all gratifying results of the seminar.

HANDOUT 20
STUDENT MODEL FOR PAPER VII: PARODY

THE MIDDLE OF SOMETHING
(A Nick Adams story)

by Louise Milkman

Up in Michigan Nick, his mother, and his father had a cabin. By the
cabin was a lake. Across the lake were Indians. There was grass around
the lake. There was also a stream. In the stream were fish. Some of the
fish were trout. The fact that some of the fish were trout is irrelevant,
but a reader may wonder what kind of fish some of the fish were and not
knowing would upset the reader and he would be upset and feel ignorant and
wonder what kind of fish was in the stream, the stream which he didn't
even know the name of but which was, by the way, the Big Two-Kidneyed
River, and the reader would lose his self-respect and know that the world
breaks everyone and afterward many are strong in the broken places and
besides, man is not made for defeat. So Nick was always very happy and
satisfied to fish or do anything well. This was the case one morning.

One morning, it was morning. The sun rose. This did not surprise
Nick because the sun often behaved that way in the morning. Nick was
used to such things. The three boys ate breakfast. They often ate
breakfast in the morning as the sun rose. They sat there eating and the
sun would rise. This usually occurred in the morning. Except when Nick
had seen an Indian cut his throat the night before and he couldn't eat.

There were three boys: Nick, his friend Bill, and his other friend,
Bill. All Nick's friends were named Bill except one who was named Wemedge.
Nick was eating oatmeal. He ate oatmeal every morning as the sun rose

1

2

(which it often did in the morning). The oatmeal was in a bowl which had oatmeal in it. It was good oatmeal. Nick reflected on the various oatmeals he had had and he knew good oatmeal when he saw it. Or tasted it. There was oatmeal and there was oatmeal. Nick knew that. Nick had a spoon with which he ate the oatmeal. He used this spoon every morning as the sun rose. He put the spoon in the bowl. It went in the oatmeal. It was obviously a Code Spoon since it could maintain grace under oatmeal. However, as Nick knew, this spoon could never compete with bullfighters. He pictured the spoon fighting a bull. It was funny. He laughed. He laughed and laughed. Did he laugh. What is funnier than a spoon in a bull ring chasing a bull. He shared his humor with Bill and Bill. He couldn't share it with Wemedge because Wemedge was not there. Bill laughed. So did Bill.

"That's one for the medical journal, George," said Nick.

But he began to be hungry. He could not remember a time when he had been so hungry. He lifted the spoon out of the bowl which had oatmeal in it. Keeping the oatmeal in the spoon, he drew the spoon towards his mouth. He kept the round part level so he would not drop the oatmeal. This took deep concentration on Nick's part and he sweated into the oatmeal. But Nick did not mind salty oatmeal. Using all the muscles of his right hand Nick carefully lifted the spoon which had oatmeal in it up to his mouth. Thus, he had transferred the oatmeal from the bowl to his mouth. Nick was very proud. It reminded him of black grasshoppers.

"Speaking of black grasshoppers," Nick said, "I saw a brown cockroach today. Boy, was he brown."

"Yes, I know what you mean," Bill said, "I saw a cockroach and it was so brown."

"There's nothing like brown cockroaches," said Bill.

3

"Except black grasshoppers," Nick said. Bill got angry. He said, "You just don't appreciate true brownness when you see it."

"Oh, boy," Nick exclaimed. Every once in a while Nick felt like exclaiming, "Oh, boy."

Bill went on talking to Bill. "Bill," Bill said to Bill, "You oughta see those brown cockroaches. They're quite brown and when there are a lot of them they look very brown."

Bill said, "Well, if we are going to brag, I knocked a whole bunch of ants off a log into a fire once."

"No," Bill said, "that was Frederic Henry."

"Oh," said Bill. Wemedge didn't comment. He couldn't because he wasn't there.

Nick wanted action. He threw some sweaty oatmeal at Bill. Bill said, "I'll kill you."

But in the early morning, sitting there by his oatmeal with his father in the next room, Nick felt quite sure he would never die.

Instructor's Comments

This student writer had fun and wants to share it with the seminar. After six papers and a great deal of seminar interaction, she is ready for parody. Her eye and ear have caught the Hemingway style--the plots, the characters, the repetitions, the length of line, the dialogue, the simple sentences with few adjectives or adverbs. By twisting a title and combining a few plots and characters, as well as adding a dash of absurdity and a heavy Hemingway theme, she has also completed the seminar. Was her parody built out of criticism? Was it a chance at last to attack and yet be praised for her skill? Or was it an exercise in creative skill? Her success as a parody writer leaves those questions unanswered.

HANDOUT 21
SEMINAR EVALUATION

1. When you first began this course, what did you think it would be about?

2. Now that you have finished this course, how would you describe it to students who are interested in taking it?

3. This course has been described as a *process* course, not just a course about one author. Do you agree with this statement? If you do, explain what this means for students beginning the course.

4. What did you enjoy *most* in this course?

5. What did you enjoy *least* in this course?

6. Write any suggestions or comments that would be useful to the instructor and to students who may take a course of this nature in the future.

APPENDIXES

APPENDIX A
A TELEPHONE CALL
TO MARY HEMINGWAY

Tuesday, April 29, 1975. 8:30 a.m. C.S.T.

It was a Big Day for the first period American literature seminar at West High School in Iowa City, Iowa. Mary Hemingway had agreed to a telephone interview from her apartment in New York City.

What's so exciting about a telephone interview? Well, let's go back a month, to early March, when my twelve juniors and seniors had already written their papers on the Nick Adams stories and *The Sun Also Rises.* After two students had completed their oral defenses of their position papers on the latter novel, Stoney—a bright eager junior—said, "I wonder what Ernest Hemingway was *really* like. I mean, after we finish *A Farewell to Arms* we have to write a paper on both the writer and the man. The stuff I've been reading in Carlos Baker's biography is good but . . . "

Connie nodded in agreement. "Wouldn't it be neat if we could talk to somebody that knew him?" she said.

I thought for a moment as the rest of the class said something about taking an extended field trip to Oak Park, Key West, Ketchum—and Cuba, if Castro were willing.

"Well, let's see . . . we have some money in the audio-visual budget for telephone calls," I said. "I've never tried that."

The class laughed. "Not that much money," said Dan.

"Wait a minute," I said. "I'm referring to the telephone kit our school has leased from Ma Bell. It's a two-way thing where the whole class can both talk and listen. We have the kit up in the A-V Center."

"Great!" shouted Dan. "Let's call someone. But who?"

"How about Mary Hemingway?" said Stoney. "You know, his wife. The last one. She has all the rights to his books and everything. Ernest used to call her 'Miss Mary.'"

"Hey, Stoney, you have been reading ahead," said Dan.

So we did. Or rather, I told the class that I had better write Mrs. Hemingway a letter to see if she would agree. On second thought, the class began to expect the worst. Someone famous talking to a high school class in *Iowa!* Indeed! But I wrote anyway, and in less than a week, Mary Hemingway sent back my letter in the self-addressed en-velope. At the bottom, she wrote, "OK." But "may the questions be specific." She noted her private phone number and suggested the best time and days of the week for an interview.

When I told the seminar about the good news, a kind of frenzy broke out. "I don't believe it. Gosh, now that we can really do it, what are we going to ask?" said Stoney.

"It was your idea in the first place," said Connie.

"We had better know something about Mrs. Hemingway," said Dan.

"We had better know something about Hemingway!" shouted Jeremy, who had just written a paper entitled "Grace Under Pressure."

We laid the groundwork for the interview. We decided to hold off the paper on *A Farewell to Arms;* we would go into biographical material about the Nobel Prize winner. With this study and the interview, the next paper on the writer would be especially meaningful. So we built up a class library of Hemingway biography, as well as articles by and about Mary Hemingway. In fact, the next day we studied a capsule biography on Mrs. Hemingway which appeared in our library issue of *Current Biography.*

It was soon obvious that Mary Hemingway was more than just the wife of an author. A noted World War II correspondent, she had met Ernest in London in 1944; he had proposed to her in a week. Ten years after their marriage and two years after the Nobel Prize, Ernest himself described his wife's many talents:

> Miss Mary is durable. She is also brave, charming, witty, exciting to look at, a pleasure to be with and a good wife. She is also an excellent fisherman, a fair wing shot, a strong swimmer, a really good cook, a good judge of wine, an excellent gardener, an amateur astronomer, a student of art, political economy, Swahili, French and Italian and can run a boat or a household in Spanish. She can also sing well. . . .

Finally, each student planned one question to ask Mary Hemingway; we also added some consensus class questions. And when we were finished, about a week before the interview, we mailed her our questions as well as a reminder of the time and date—especially the time since we were on Central Standard Time. My assessment of our questions: she would need about six hours to answer them. Maybe more. Yet we had a half-hour of budgeted telephone time.

But we were ready. So we thought.

The day of the interview was a comedy of frenzy, errors, and delight. Obviously untrained in the science of interview, we hooked up the telephone kit in the office conference room. Nervous—we called one student's home three times to make sure the phone was working. About the only intelligent planning was a last-minute discussion of whether we should tape the interview. Somebody screamed something about Watergate. Another said he had checked with the A-V director who said we would need a beeper as well as written permission from Mrs. Hemingway. So no tape recording.

In desperation, wanting to have some record, some expert note-taking, we asked a school secretary to take shorthand notes. Later, we discovered that she had been so flustered by the obvious excitement and tension in the conference room that she did not get one sentence on paper!

Aside from this, the interview went perfectly. Everybody asked a question; everybody spoke to "Miss Mary." Each student was absolutely satisfied with her responses —always to the point, never ducking an issue, complete with anecdotes, kind, and so very alive and intelligent. During the interview, I looked across the room with delight as everybody seemed to be nodding and smiling and taking notes.

When our half-hour was up, everybody shouted—oh, so unsophisticated but oh, so natural—"Goodbye! Goodbye . . . and thanks!"

The next day we pooled our notes, our memories.

"She *really* answered my question about how she felt when she and Ernest were in those two airplane crashes in Africa," said Marzia.

"What did she say?" groaned Dan, who had missed the interview because of the flu.

"She said, 'Try it sometime. And you'll know,'" laughed Marzia.

"Did anybody ask my question about what Ernest's routine was down in Cuba and whether she ever talked with him about his writing when he was working?" said Dan.

"I did," said Will. "She said he was at work fairly steady, usually from seven to twelve in the morning. She said he didn't talk much about his writing even though she typed the manuscript of *The Old Man and the Sea*. But she did say that she had told him she hoped he wouldn't kill off the Old Man at the end."

Then Greg, a serious National Merit winner, began to review what Mary had said about literary criticism. "She said she wasn't a critic, but she did say she had a fond-

ness for *The Sun Also Rises* because it seemed like a vital and true book about the special craziness of Paris in the 1920s. And she loved the way Ernest had dealt with the beautiful scenery of Spain—and the bullfights in Pamplona."

"Hey, Greg, don't forget that Mary said that picking her favorite book is like asking a mother which of her seven children she likes best," said Stoney.

"Right," said Greg. "I guess you could sum up the whole point about literary criticism by saying that she felt Hemingway was largely unconcerned about critics. He didn't write to prove himself—certainly not with *The Old Man and the Sea*. He was a writer who wrote about what interested him."

During our discussion, we began to piece together the rest of the interview into a kind of *U.S. News and World Report* format:

Cheryl: "Why do you think many Communist countries like Ernest's writings?"

M. H.: "I'm not sure. But the Russians compare him to Shakespeare. Though we see the royalties piling up in Russia, we can't take any money out. Of course, they never liked *For Whom the Bell Tolls*."

Stoney: "What were Ernest's political and racial views?"

M. H.: "Ernest was apolitical. He lived much of his life outside the United States. As for prejudices, he had none. Our friends included Orientals and blacks. For example, one of our good friends was a black boxer who used to live in our home in Cuba."

Charles: "Where did Ernest get his ideas for the so-called 'Code Hero,' the man who could endure the hardships of life?"

M. H.: "I think he lived the life of the Code Hero because he believed in grace under pressure, in courage. Those important values were taught to him by his Victorian background back in Oak Park, Illinois."

Connie: "I read that one of the most important assets that a woman friend of Ernest Hemingway can have is *durability*. What were some of the things about him that made this true?"

M. H. (laughing): "Oh, that was something I had said as kind of a joke. We had been down in Peru doing some fishing under pretty rugged circumstances. The weather and the ocean were rough. I had said something about how you had to be 'durable' to go fishing with Ernest. Later, he repeated that line."

Janie: "What were Ernest's personal tastes in such things as favorite writers, clothing, food, automobiles, and movies?"

M. H.: "Ernest had lots of favorite writers—oh, Tolstoi, Twain, Balzac, and Shakespeare's *King Lear*.

He wasn't much on clothing, though he was sensitive to texture. That's something that's not been noted about him. He especially loved texture in food, especially Chinese food. And he loved spicey food, too ... He loved convertibles, always had one. He saw few movies, though I do remember how much he liked *Around the World in 80 Days*."

Class: "Are you planning to release any more of his unpublished writing?"

M. H.: "Maybe. But it *must* always be up to his best standards. Nothing must be added. We still are considering "Dangerous Summer" and a long amorphous book called "Garden of Eden.""

As we sat there, transcribing our notes and heading into the next Hemingway paper, a kind of euphoria settled over the room. A special kind of confidence—though admittedly bolstered by only a brief and fragmentary telephone call—prevailed. But it was a telephone call to remember for the rest of your life.

APPENDIX B
THE LIFE AND TIMES
OF ERNEST HEMINGWAY

Ernest Hemingway	The Times

THE EARLY YEARS (1899-1919)

1899

Hemingway born on July 21 in Oak Park, Illinois, second of six children of Dr. Clarence and Grace Hall Hemingway.

U.S. population: 75,994,575. McKinley administration (1897-1901). Taft (1909-1913). Model T mass produced (1909).

1914-18

Summers at Windemere in Northern Michigan.

World War I (1914-18). Wilson administration (1913-1921). Panama Canal opens.

1917

Graduation from Oak Park High School. Reporter for Kansas City *Star*. Rejected by U.S. Army for bad eye.

U.S. in World War I. Caporetto campaigns begin in Italy.

1918

Red Cross ambulance driver in Italy. Wounded near Fossalta di Piave, July 8. Love affair with Agnes von Kurowsky.

Armistice, November 1918, ending World War I. Wilson's Fourteen Points.

1919

In Petoskey, Michigan, the "Big Two-Hearted River" country, writing.

Treaty of Versailles. Sherwood Anderson, *Winesburg, Ohio*. Volstead Prohibition Act.

THE PARIS PERIOD (1920-1927)

1920-24

Reporter for Toronto *Star* and *Star Weekly*. Life in Paris. Meets Gertrude Stein. Marriage to Hadley (1921). John ("Bumby") born (1923).

F. Scott Fitzgerald, *This Side of Paradise* (1920). The Roaring 20s. Harding administration (1921-1923). Sacco and Vanzetti trial (1921).

1921-24

Foreign correspondent for Toronto papers. First war correspondence, Graeco-Turkish War (1922).

Graeco-Turkish War (1921-1922). James Joyce, *Ulysses* (1922). T. S. Eliot, *The Waste Land* (1922).

1923

Three Stories and Ten Poems, Paris. Contains "Up in Michigan," "Out of Season," "My Old Man."

U.S. population over 105 million. Coolidge administration (1923-1929). Teapot Dome Scandal (1923-1924).

1924

in our time, Paris, thirty-two pages. Contains "Indian Camp."

1925

In Our Time, first Hemingway book published in U.S., Boni & Liveright publishers. Adds fourteen short stories to the miniatures, now interchapters, of *in our time.*

Fitzgerald, *The Great Gatsby.* Anderson, *Dark Laughter.* Scopes "Monkey" trial.

1926

Torrents of Spring, parody of Anderson's *Dark Laughter. The Sun Also Rises* (British title: *Fiesta*).

Transatlantic wireless telephone. Byrd flies over North Pole.

1927

Men Without Women, fourteen short stories (ten of which had appeared in magazines). Divorce from Hadley, marriage to Pauline Pfeiffer.

Charles Lindbergh flies from New York to Paris in Spirit of St. Louis.

KEY WEST PERIOD (1927–1940)

1928

Birth of son Patrick. Moves to Key West, Florida. Father commits suicide in Oak Park.

Talking movies, first Mickey Mouse cartoon.

1929

A Farewell to Arms, first commercial success: 80,000 copies sold in four months.

Stock market crash. William Faulkner, *The Sound and the Fury.* Hoover administration (1929–1933).

1931

Birth of son Gregory.

1932

Death in the Afternoon, nonfiction work on bullfighting.

U.S. population over 122 million. Ford's 20 millionth car. FDR elected (1933–1945).

1933

Winner Take Nothing, fourteen short stories. Writes for *Esquire,* first of thirty-one articles for magazine over next six years.

Depression. FDR's CCC, TVA, NRA, AAA. Hitler, German Chancellor.

1934

Purchases *Pilar,* thirty-eight-foot cruiser, fishing.

Mao's Long March in China.

1935

Green Hills of Africa, nonfiction work about big-game hunting.

Italy invades Ethiopia. WPA. Regular transpacific air service.

1936

Writes, speaks, raises money for Loyalists in Spanish Civil War.

Spanish Civil War, Franco vs. Loyalists.

1937

In Spain covering civil war for Northern American Newspaper Alliance. Film work on *The Spanish Earth. To Have and Have Not,* three interconnected stories, two of which had been published separately.

CIO sitdown strike. Japan invades China.

1938

The Fifth Column and the First Forty-Nine Stories. Contains a play, stories from previous collections, and seven stories previously published in magazines.

Thorton Wilder, *Our Town.* Pearl Buck wins Nobel Prize. Hitler and Chamberlain meet at Munich Conference.

1939

Ernest and Pauline separate. Ernest moves to Finca Vigia estate, fifteen miles from Havana, Cuba.

World War II begins; Germany attacks Poland. John Steinbeck, *The Grapes of Wrath.*

THE WAR PERIOD (1940–1945)

1940

For Whom the Bell Tolls, his best-selling novel. Divorced by Pauline; marries Martha Gellhorn.

U.S. population 131 million. New York World's Fair closes. Nazi bombing of Britain.

1941

Goes to China as war correspondent.

December 7, Japanese bomb Pearl Harbor. U.S. enters World War II.

1942

Pilar patrols Caribbean for U-boats. *Men at War,* collection of war stories and accounts.

U.S. Air Force bombs Europe, naval battles in Pacific.

1943–45

Covers European Theater of war as newspaper and magazine correspondent. Divorced by Martha Gellhorn (1944). Marries Mary Welsh.

D-Day, V-E, V-J Days. Atomic Age begins. U.N. Charter. Death of FDR. Truman administration (1945–1952).

THE CUBAN PERIOD (1945–1960)

1948–49

Interviewed by Malcolm Cowley. Allows first biographical study for *Life.*

Norman Mailer, *The Naked and the Dead* (1948). Berlin Airlift (1948).

1950

Across the River and into the Trees, much criticized novel.

Korean War begins. McCarthy era.

1951

Death of Hemingway's mother.

J. D. Salinger, *Catcher in the Rye.*

1952

The Old Man and the Sea, first published in *Life.* Pulitzer Prize.

Ralph Ellison, *Invisible Man.* Eisenhower administration (1952-60).

1954

Nobel Prize for Literature. Cited for "forceful and style-making mastery of the art of modern narration." Injured in two airplane crashes in Africa.

Supreme Court rules racial segregation unconstitutional.

1956

Filming of *The Old Man and the Sea* as Hemingway observes.

Israeli-Egyptian War.

1957-58

Works on Paris memoirs.

1959

Buys hunting lodge near Ketchum, Idaho.   Cuban Revolution and rise of Fidel Castro.

KETCHUM, IDAHO (1960-1961), AND POSTHUMOUS

1960-61

Onset of breakdown. Hospitalization in Rochester, Minnesota, at Mayo Clinic (1960). Begins a bullfighting story, "The Dangerous Summer."   First jet passenger service. Kennedy administration (1960-63).

1961

Death on July 2 of self-inflicted gunshot wounds.   Alan Shepard's suborbital space flight.

1964

A Moveable Feast—Paris memoirs.

1967

By-Line: Ernest Hemingway—selected news writings.

1970

Islands in the Stream.

THE HEMINGWAY FAMILY

Ernest Miller Hemingway

Born July 21, 1899, in Oak Park, Illinois, the second oldest child of Clarence and Grace Hemingway. Died July 2, 1961, in Ketchum, Idaho, of self-inflicted gunshot wounds.

Grandparents

Anson T. Hemingway

Adelaide Edmonds Hemingway

Ernest Miller Hall

Caroline Hancock Hall

Parents

Dr. Clarence Edmonds Hemingway: died of self-inflicted gunshot wounds in 1928 in Oak Park, Illinois.

Grace Hall Hemingway: died in 1951 at the age of seventy-nine in Memphis, Tennessee.

Brother and Sisters

Marcelline (born 1898)

Ursula (born 1902)

Madelaine "Sunny" (born 1904)

Carol (born 1911)

Leicester (born 1915)

Wives and Children

Hadley Richardson (marriage: 1921-1927)
    Son: John "Bumby" (born 1923)
Pauline Pfeiffer (marriage: 1927-1940)
    Sons: Patrick (born 1928)
            Gregory (born 1931)
Martha Gellhorn (marriage: 1940-1944)
Mary Welsh (marriage: 1944-1961)

APPENDIX C
ANECDOTES FROM
THE HEMINGWAY BIOGRAPHY

The following seven anecdotes are included in this handbook to initiate the profile discussion. For those students and teachers who have difficulty locating reference materials in their school or community, these anecdotes are offered as models, resources, alternates for a large group discussion, or whatever seems most useful.

ANECDOTE 1

Ernest Hemingway liked boxing. Though his father had taught him to enjoy outdoor sports such as hunting and fishing, Ernest began to box when he was in high school. When the coast was clear, he and his friends would engage in vigorous one-round bouts in his family's Oak Park, Illinois, music room where he was supposed to be practicing on his cello. Even though his father had a horror of physical violence, Ernest would take boxing lessons at a Chicago gym.

Later in the 1920s, Hemingway would continue boxing workouts in Paris. One of his most memorable matches was with Morley Callaghan, another American expatriate author.

Ernest and Morley would go to the American Club. At first, Callaghan was plenty worried, being only five eight and overweight, plus being aware of the story that Ernest had flattened the French middleweight champion. Ernest became frustrated with Morley's poor style, but Callaghan gained confidence with each punch.

One dark cloudy morning, Callaghan caught Ernest with a solid left to the mouth. Hemingway's mouth began to bleed. Then Ernest caught another punch, which made him furious at the sight of his own blood. He spat in Callaghan's face and on his shirt. Shocked, Callaghan stopped fighting. They stared at each other. Then Ernest said, "That's what bullfighters do when they're wounded. It's a way of showing contempt." Then Hemingway smiled, was friendly and sweet again. Callaghan always wondered about that match. Was it all pure theater? [Source: Carlos Baker, *Ernest Hemingway: A Life Story*, pp. 22–23; Morley Callaghan, *That Summer in Paris*, pp. 97–100, 118–22.]

ANECDOTE 2

Ernest Hemingway was accident-prone all his life. While amateur psychologists might call it part of his death wish, others remember how bravely he bore with these accidents, his "grace under pressure." One of his earliest accidents was remembered by his younger brother Leicester.

In the summer, the Hemingway family would leave their Oak Park home and go to northern Michigan near Walloon Lake, the setting of Ernest's "Up in Michigan" stories. They had a cottage where Dr. Hemingway would relax. The entire family loved the woods and the fishing. The children had errands too, Ernest's being a daily milk run to the Bacon farm about a half mile away. On one of these errands to bring home milk, Ernest had a bad accident.

One morning as he ran off to get the milk, carrying a short stick, he stumbled near a ravine and fell forward. The stick was driven into the back of his throat into both tonsils. Blood gushed forth as he rushed back to the cottage for treatment. As his father stanched the blood, Ernest remained stoic though his mother was horrified. The throat remained tender for some time, and his father told him to whistle whenever he felt like crying. Leicester later remembered that he saw a photograph of Ernest at an Italian hospital recuperating from numerous mortar wounds: Ernest was whistling through clenched teeth. [Source: Leicester Hemingway, *My Brother*, pp. 19–22.]

ANECDOTE 3

Ernest covered the 1922 Lausanne Peace Conference in Switzerland while his wife Hadley nursed a cold in Paris. While at the conference, he kept pleading that she fly down and join him. Finally, Hadley agreed to come by train, rushed down to the station, and made a journey that biographer Carlos Baker called "so horrible for Ernest that neither of them was ever able to forget it."

Hadley had decided to take all of Ernest's manuscripts in a separate small valise so that he could get on with his writing during the Christmas holiday. Except for two stories, "Up in Michigan" and "My Old Man," she brought all the fiction and poetry that she could find.

When Hadley left their Paris apartment, she took a taxi to the Gare de Lyon and there secured a porter to carry the luggage to the train compartment. Somehow the valise with the manuscripts disappeared as she boarded to travel south. The trip was one of horror. When she arrived, Ernest listened to her tale of woe amidst a vale of tears. He later wrote how he rushed back to Paris in hopes that the carbons had been left behind. But they had been in the valise too. [Source: Carlos Baker, *Ernest Hemingway: A Life Story*, pp. 102-3.]

ANECDOTE 4

In the mid-1930s, Ernest Hemingway was living in Key West, Florida, with his second wife Pauline. Besides writing, Ernest would hang around Sloppy Joe's Bar or take his Mob fishing for marlin with his thirty-eight-footer, the diesel-powered *Pilar*. People began to call him "Papa," and a kind of myth was built around him.

At least two good stories came from this period.

The first was at Sloppy Joe's where one of his drinking companions named George Brooks, a local attorney, enjoyed making Hemingway miserable. Brooks's favorite trick was with homosexuals who came in the bar in search for sailors. One day he told a young man that Hemingway was "as queer as a three dollar bill." Then he said, "Just go up to him and give him a big kiss and tell him you love him." When the young man did, Ernest turned white as a ghost, then spat and knocked the guy cold with a right punch. Turning to George Brooks, he said, "I know you're behind this you conniving son-of-a-bitch, I know it." George denied it, innocently insisting the poor devil was a genuine fan of the great Ernest Hemingway.

The second story is a fish story. One April Sunday in 1935, Papa was trolling the Gulf Stream on the way to Bimini. He sighted a large green turtle, and he and two companions then got simultaneous strikes. Ernest pulled his line first, a large shark. Holding the shark in position alongside with the gaff in his left hand and his Colt in the right, Hemingway began to pump bullets into the shark's head. Suddenly the gaff broke and Hemingway found himself with legs all covered with blood. Somehow, he had managed to shoot himself in both legs! "Dammit," he told his brother who theorized the damage came from the ricochet, "That's one for the books." [Source: Leicester Hemingway, *My Brother*, p. 164; McLendon, *Papa*, pp. 152-53.]

ANECDOTE 5

When Ernest Hemingway's temper was roused, he was inclined to punch out his adversary. Around Easter of 1936, the poet Wallace Stevens had the misfortune of arousing the Oak Park boxer-author.

Stevens, a portly Hartford insurance executive and some twenty years Hemingway's senior, had the myopia to make negative remarks about Hemingway at a Key West cocktail party to Hemingway's sister Sunny. She had just completed the arduous task of typing *A Farewell to Arms* for her brother and then had to come to Ernest's defense as Stevens pressed the criticism. Stevens' remark that she had little literary insight sent her home near tears.

When Sunny told Ernest, he rushed out of his house and drove to the party. The genteel members of the soiree were horrified to discover Ernest calling Stevens outside and then proceeding to break the poet's jaw with a vicious left hook. After that Ernest went into what he called "hiding from the law," while Stevens lay in pain at the local Marine Hospital, receiving nourishment through a straw in his wired jaw.

Later, Hemingway felt badly about the matter, partly because he knew that he was open to a case of assault and battery. But Stevens had kept quiet and when he was released, he showed up at Hemingway's South Street front door—and again announced his displeasure with Hemingway's prose though he did apologize for insulting Sunny. Ernest was impressed with the spunk of the "little squirt" and invited Stevens in for a drink. The matter ended there, kept from public attention. [Source: McLendon, *Papa*, pp. 55-57.]

ANECDOTE 6

There is an old literary chestnut about "the reports of my death being grossly exaggerated." Such was the case with Ernest Hemingway in January of 1954.

Hemingway and his wife Mary had gone to Africa for a safari and a vacation. On January 21, they climbed into Roy Marsh's Cessna 180 at the West Nairobi airport for a trip to the Belgian Congo. The first day's flight was uneventful though nostalgic as Ernest pointed out the old 1933 campsite where his former wife Pauline had killed a lion. That night they stayed at Bukava. The next day was much the same with Mary taking lots of photographs of African wildlife. But on the third day, near Murchison Falls, a flight of ibis suddenly crossed the path of the plane.

Hemingway's friend Marsh dived to avoid the ibis, struck an abandoned telephone wire, crunched to a landing about three miles from the falls. Though Mary suffered initial shock and Ernest a sprained right shoulder, no one was badly hurt. But they didn't receive any response to their "Mayday" pleas.

Luckily, they spotted a large white boat on a nearby river. They caught a ride (and had to pay the fare) to Lake Albert and Butiaba. There a bush pilot named Reggie Cartwright took them to the local airport for a trip to Entebbe. As the plane taxied across the badly plowed field, it suddenly burst into flames as it attempted to rise. Ernest smashed his way through the jammed cabin door as Mary managed to escape through the port side. Mary had a damaged knee, Ernest a bleeding scalp. A local policeman rescued them and took them fifty miles to Masindi to the Railway Hotel. The next day a doctor arrived, and they were transported a hundred miles away to the Lake Victoria Hotel.

The next morning the whole place was buzzing with the press who had learned of the first wreck and announced to the world that Ernest Hemingway was dead. Mary cabled her parents while Ernest began to recuperate from a collapsed intestine, kidney trouble, an aching backbone, and a head like an egg. Roy Marsh got a Cessna to take Hemingway to Nairobi.

Only nine days had passed, but Hemingway had experienced two air crashes, multiple injuries. Ernest read the host of premature obituaries with what Mary called "immortal zest." He also wondered how many people had welcomed the news of his "death." [Source: Carlos Baker, *Ernest Hemingway: A Life Story*, pp. 518-22.]

ANECDOTE 7

When Ernest Hemingway was found dead on July 2, 1961, at his Ketchum, Idaho, lodge, some people insisted that he had died from an accident. They said that the "incredible accident" was caused while Ernest was cleaning his favorite shotgun. Few people think such things today.

Ernest's ideas about death go back as early as 1918 when he wrote his parents from Italy where he had been badly wounded. He wrote them that death was a very simple thing because he had seen it and knew. As a young man, he feared the time when his body was old, worn out, when his illusions might be shattered. Close readers of his works from *A Farewell to Arms* to *To Have and Have Not* trace these early ideas about death.

They also point out that Hemingway's father committed suicide with a gun.

The events just before his suicide belie that death was accidental. For over a year, the strain of poor health took its toll. He began to worry about money, about his telephones being bugged by the federal government, about going crazy, about his blood pressure. In December of 1960, he was admitted to the Rochester, Minnesota, Mayo Clinic and given eleven treatments with electric shock. After he left the Clinic, he became even less communicative, and by April of 1961, Mary saw that a great sadness had come over him: he couldn't write. One morning at Ketchum she found him in his bathrobe holding his shotgun.

Then events began to mount: (1) Just before he was to return to Rochester, a friend wrestled his loaded shotgun from him as he held it to his throat. (2) At a refueling stop at the Rapid City airport, he went looking for a gun in the hangar. (3) At Rapid City, he tried to walk into the propeller of another plane. (4) At Rochester, he promised his doctor not to commit suicide. And then in June, he convinced the doctors that he was fit to go back to Ketchum.

Mary Hemingway knew that a mistake had been made in letting him go back to Ketchum, but when they reached the lodge on Friday, June 30, she hoped for the best. On Sunday morning, she found him dead with a double-barreled Boss shotgun that he used for pigeon hunting. [Source: Leicester Hemingway, *My Brother*, p. 256; Carlos Baker, *Ernest Hemingway: A Life Story*, pp. 199, 554-64; Hotchner, *Papa Hemingway: A Personal Memoir*, pp. 264-304.]

APPENDIX D
ON THE BLUE WATER:
A GULF STREAM LETTER

Ernest Hemingway

Certainly there is no hunting like the hunting of man and those who have hunted armed men long enough and liked it, never really care for anything else thereafter. You will meet them doing various things with resolve, but their interest rarely holds because after the other thing ordinary life is as flat as the taste of wine when the taste buds have been burned off your tongue. Wine, when your tongue has been burned clean with lye and water, feels like puddle water in your mouth, while mustard feels like axle-grease, and you can smell crisp, fried bacon, but when you taste it, there is only a feeling of crinkly lard.

You can learn about this matter of the tongue by coming into the kitchen of a villa on the Riviera late at night and taking a drink from what should be a bottle of Evian water and which turns out to be *Eau de Javel*, a concentrated lye product used for cleaning sinks. The taste buds on your tongue, if burned off by *Eau de Javel*, will begin to function again after about a week. At what rate other things regenerate one does not know, since you lose track of friends and the things one could learn in a week were mostly learned a long time ago.

The other night I was talking with a good friend to whom all hunting is dull except elephant hunting. To him there is no sport in anything unless there is great danger and, if the danger is not enough, he will increase it for his own satisfaction. A hunting companion of his had told me how this friend was not satisfied with the risks of ordinary elephant hunting but would, if possible, have the elephants driven, or turned, so he could take them head-on, so it was a choice of killing them with the difficult frontal shot as they came, trumpeting, with their ears spread, or having them run over him. This is to elephant hunting what the German cult of suicide climbing is to ordinary mountaineering, and I suppose it is, in a way, an attempt to approximate the old hunting of the armed man who is hunting you.

This friend was speaking of elephant hunting and urging me to hunt elephant, as he said that once you took it up no other hunting would mean anything to you. I was arguing that I enjoyed all hunting and shooting, any sort I could get, and had no desire to wipe this capacity for enjoyment out with the *Eau de Javel* of the old elephant coming straight at you with his trunk up and his ears spread.

"Of course you like that big fishing too," he said rather sadly. "Frankly, I can't see where the excitement is in that."

"You'd think it was marvelous if the fish shot at you with Tommy guns or jumped back and forth through the cockpit with swords on the ends of their noses."

"Don't be silly," he said. "But frankly I don't see where the thrill is."

"Look at so and so," I said. "He's an elephant hunter and this last year he's gone fishing for big fish and he's goofy about it. He must get a kick out of it or he wouldn't do it."

"Yes," my friend said. "There must be something about it but I can't see it. Tell me where you get a thrill out of it."

"I'll try to write it in a piece sometime," I told him.

"I wish you would," he said. "Because you people are sensible on other subjects. Moderately sensible I mean."

"I'll write it."

In the first place, the Gulf Stream and the other great ocean currents are the last wild country there is left. Once you are out of sight of land and of the other boats you are more alone than you can ever be hunting and the sea is the same as it has been since before men ever went on it in boats. In a season fishing you will see it oily flat as the becalmed galleons saw it while they drifted to the westward; white-capped with a fresh breeze as they saw it running with the trades; and in high, rolling blue hills the tops blowing off them like

103

snow as they were punished by it, so that sometimes you will see three great hills of water with your fish jumping from the top of the farthest one and if you tried to make a turn to go with him without picking your chance, one of those breaking crests would roar down in on you with a thousand tons of water and you would hunt no more elephants, Richard, my lad.

There is no danger from the fish, but anyone who goes on the sea the year around in a small power boat does not seek danger. You may be absolutely sure that in a year you will have it without seeking, so you try always to avoid it all you can.

Because the Gulf Stream is an unexploited country, only the very fringe of it ever being fished, and then only at a dozen places in thousands of miles of current, no one knows what fish live in it, or how great size they reach or what age, or even what kinds of fish and animals live in it at different depths. When you are drifting, out of sight of land, fishing four lines, sixty, eighty, one hundred and one hundred fifty fathoms down, in water that is seven hundred fathoms deep you never know what may take the small tuna that you use for bait, and every time the line starts to run off the reel, slowly first, then with a scream of the click as the rod bends and you feel it double and the huge weight of the friction of the line rushing through that depth of water while you pump and reel, pump and reel, pump and reel, trying to get the belly out of the line before the fish jumps, there is always a thrill that needs no danger to make it real. It may be a marlin that will jump high and clear off to your right and then go off in a series of leaps, throwing a splash like a speedboat in a sea as you shout for the boat to turn with him watching the line melting off the reel before the boat can get around. Or it may be a broadbill that will show wagging his great broadsword. Or it may be some fish that you will never see at all that will head straight out to the northwest like a submerged submarine and never show and at the end of five hours the angler has a straightened-out hook. There is always a feeling of excitement when a fish takes hold when you are drifting deep.

In hunting you know what you are after and the top you can get is an elephant. But who can say what you will hook sometime when drifting in a hundred and fifty fathoms in the Gulf Stream? There are probably marlin and swordfish to which the fish we have seen caught are pygmies; and every time a fish takes the bait drifting you have a feeling perhaps you are hooked to one of these.

Carlos, our Cuban mate, who is fifty-three years old and has been fishing for marlin since he went in the bow of a skiff with his father when he was seven, was fishing drifting deep one time when he hooked a white marlin. The fish jumped twice and then sounded and when he sounded suddenly Carlos felt a great weight and he could not hold the line which went out and down and down irresistibly until the fish had taken out over a hundred

and fifty fathoms. Carlos says it felt as heavy and solid as though he were hooked to the bottom of the sea. Then suddenly the strain was loosened but he could feel the weight of his original fish and pulled it up stone dead. Some toothless fish like a swordfish or marlin had closed his jaws across the middle of the eighty pound white marlin and squeezed it and held it so that every bit of the insides of the fish had been crushed out while the huge fish moved off with the eighty-pound fish in its mouth. Finally it let go. What size of a fish would that be? I thought it might be a giant squid but Carlos said there were no sucker marks on the fish and that it showed plainly the shape of the marlin's mouth where he had crushed it.

Another time an old man fishing alone in a skiff out of Cabañas hooked a great marlin that, on the heavy sashcord handline, pulled the skiff far out to sea. Two days later the old man was picked up by fishermen sixty miles to the eastward, the head and forward part of the marlin lashed alongside. What was left of the fish, less than half, weighed eight hundred pounds. The old man had stayed with him a day, a night, a day and another night while the fish swam deep and pulled the boat. When he had come up the old man had pulled the boat up on him and harpooned him. Lashed alongside the sharks had hit him and the old man had fought them out alone in the Gulf Stream in a skiff, clubbing them, stabbing at them, lunging at them with an oar until he was exhausted and the sharks had eaten all that they could hold. He was crying in the boat when the fishermen picked him up, half crazy from his loss, and the sharks were still circling the boat.

But what is the excitement in catching them from a launch? It comes from the fact that they are strange and wild things of unbelievable speed and power and a beauty, in the water and leaping, that is indescribable, which you would never see if you did not fish for them, and to which you are suddenly harnessed so that you feel their speed, their force and their savage power as intimately as if you were riding a bucking horse. For half an hour, an hour, or five hours, you are fastened to the fish as much as he is fastened to you and you tame him and break him the way a wild horse is broken and finally lead him to the boat. For pride and because the fish is worth plenty of money in the Havana market, you gaff him at the boat and bring him on board, but the having him in the boat isn't the excitement; it is while you are fighting him that is the fun.

If the fish is hooked in the bony part of the mouth I am sure the hook hurts him no more than the harness hurts the angler. A large fish when he is hooked often does not feel the hook at all and will swim toward the boat, unconcerned, to take another bait. At other times he will swim away deep, completely unconscious of the hook, and it is when he feels himself held and pressure exerted to turn him, that he knows something is wrong and starts to make his fight. Unless he is hooked where it hurts he makes his fight not against the pain of the hook, but against being captured and if, when he is out of sight, you figure what he is doing, in what direction he is pulling when deep down, and why, you can convince him and bring him to the boat by the same system you break a wild horse. It is not necessary to kill him, or even completely exhaust him to bring him to the boat.

To kill a fish that fights deep you pull against the direction he wants to go until he is worn out and dies. It takes hours and when the fish dies the sharks are liable to get him before the angler can raise him to the top. To catch such a fish quickly you figure by trying to hold him absolutely, which direction he is working (a sounding fish is going in the direction the line slants in the water when you have put enough pressure on the drag so the line would break if you held it any tighter); then get ahead of him on that direction and he can be brought to the boat without killing him. You do not tow him or pull him with the motor boat; you use the engine to shift your position just as you would walk up or down stream with a salmon. A fish is caught most surely from a small boat such as a dory since the angler can shut down on his drag and simply let the fish pull the boat. Towing the boat will kill him in time. But the most satisfaction is to dominate and convince the fish and bring him intact in everything but spirit to the boat as rapidly as possible.

"Very instructive," says the friend. "But where does the thrill come in?"

The thrill comes when you are standing at the wheel drinking a cold bottle of beer and watching the outriggers jump the baits so they look like small live tuna leaping along and then behind one you see a long dark shadow wing up and then a big spear thrust out followed by an eye and head and dorsal fin and the tuna jumps with the wave and he's missed it.

"Marlin," Carlos yells from the top of the house and stamps his feet up and down, the signal that a fish is raised. He swarms down to the wheel and you go back to where the rod rests in its socket and there comes the shadow again, fast as the shadow of a plane moving over the water, and the spear, head, fin and shoulders smash out of water and you hear the click the closepin makes as the line pulls out and the long bight of line whishes through the water as the fish turns and as you hold the rod, you feel it double and the butt kicks you in the belly as you come back hard and feel his weight, as you strike him again and again, and again.

Then the heavy rod arc-ing out toward the fish, and the reel in a band-saw zinging scream, the marlin leaps clear and long, silver in the sun long, round as a hogshead and banded with lavender stripes and, when he goes into the water, it throws a column of spray like a shell lighting.

Then he comes out again, and the spray roars, and

again, then the line feels slack and out he bursts headed across and in, then jumps wildly twice more seeming to hang high and stiff in the air before falling to throw the column of water and you can see the hook in the corner of his jaw.

Then in a series of jumps like a greyhound he heads to the northwest and standing up, you follow him in the boat, the line taut as a banjo string and little drops coming from it until you finally get the belly of it clear of that friction against the water and have a straight pull out toward the fish.

And all the time Carlos is shouting, "Oh, God the bread of my children! Oh look at the bread of my children! Joseph and Mary look at the bread of my children jump! There it goes the bread of my children! He'll never stop the bread the bread the bread of my children!"

This striped marlin jumped, in a straight line to the northwest, fifty-three times, and every time he went out it was a sight to make your heart stand still. Then he sounded and I said to Carlos, "Get me the harness. Now I've got to pull him up the bread of your children."

"I couldn't stand to see it," he says. "Like a filled pocketbook jumping. He can't go down deep now. He's caught too much air jumping."

"Like a race horse over obstacles," Julio says. "Is the harness all right? Do you want water?"

"No." Then kidding Carlos, "What's this about the bread of your children?"

"He always says that," says Julio. "You should hear him curse me when we would lose one in the skiff."

"What will the bread of your children weigh?" I ask with mouth dry, the harness taut across shoulders, the rod a flexible prolongation of the sinew pulling ache of arms, the sweat salty in my eyes.

"Four hundred and fifty," says Carlos.

"Never," says Julio.

"Thou and thy never," says Carlos. "The fish of another always weighs nothing to thee."

"Three seventy-five," Julio raises his estimate. "Not a pound more."

Carlos says something unprintable and Julio comes up to four hundred.

The fish is nearly whipped now and the dead ache is out of raising him, and then, while lifting, I feel something slip. It holds for an instant and then the line is slack.

"He's gone," I say and unbuckle the harness.

"The bread of your children," Julio says to Carlos.

"Yes," Carlos says. "Yes. Joke and no joke yes. *El pan de mis hijos.* Three hundred and fifty pounds at ten cents a pound. How many days does a man work for that in the winter? How cold is it at three o'clock in the morning on all those days? And the fog and the rain in a norther. Every time he jumps the hook cutting the hole a little bigger in his jaw. Ay how he could jump. How he could jump!"

"The bread of your children," says Julio.

"Don't talk about that any more," said Carlos.

No it is not elephant hunting. But we get a kick out of it. When you have a family and children, your family, or my family, or the family of Carlos, you do not have to look for danger. There is always plenty of danger when you have a family.

And after a while the danger of others is the only danger and there is no end to it nor any pleasure in it nor does it help to think about it.

But there is great pleasure in being on the sea, in the unknown wild suddenness of a great fish; in his life and death which he lives for you in an hour while your strength is harnessed to his; and there is satisfaction in conquering this thing which rules the sea it lives in.

Then in the morning of the day after you have caught a good fish, when the man who carried him to the market in a handcart brings the long roll of heavy silver dollars wrapped in a newspaper on board it is very satisfactory money. It really feels like money.

"There's the bread of your children," you say to Carlos.

"In the time of the dance of the millions," he says, "a fish like that was worth two hundred dollars. Now it is thirty. On the other hand a fisherman never starves. The sea is very rich."

"And the fisherman always poor."

"No. Look at you. You are rich."

"Like hell," you say. "And the longer I fish the poorer I'll be. I'll end up fishing with you for the market in a dinghy."

"That I never believe," says Carlos devoutly. "But look. That fishing in a dinghy is very interesting. You would like it."

"I'll look forward to it," you say.

"What we need for prosperity is a war," Carlos says. "In the time of the war with Spain and in the last war the fishermen were actually rich."

"All right," you say. "If we have a war you get the dinghy ready."

BIBLIOGRAPHY

BASIC MATERIALS FOR STARTING A SEMINAR

Of course, the school budget determines the quantity of materials. If there is no budget, materials can be obtained from many sources: school and public libraries, student, teacher, or classroom copies, American literature textbooks.

Class sets of paperbacks do provide smoother instruction. In addition to the handouts suggested in this book, the following materials are recommended for starting a Hemingway seminar:

Hemingway, Ernest. *A Farewell to Arms.* New York: Scribner's, 1929. Cloth and paper.

The Old Man and the Sea. New York: Scribner's, 1961. Cloth and paper.

The Short Stories of Ernest Hemingway. New York: Scribner's, 1938. Cloth and paper.

Three Novels: The Sun Also Rises, A Farewell to Arms, The Old Man and the Sea. New York: Scribner's, 1962.

The Sun Also Rises. New York: Scribner's, 1926. Cloth and paper.

Besides the class sets, the instructor may wish to build up a room library of biographical and autobiographical works. Some of these may be secured through libraries. Here is a list of eleven useful titles:

Baker, Carlos. *Ernest Hemingway: A Life Story.* New York: Scribner's, 1969.

Callaghan, Morley. *That Summer in Paris: Memories of Tangled Friendships with Hemingway, Fitzgerald, and Some Others.* New York: Coward, 1963.

Cowley, Malcolm. "A Portrait of Mister Papa." *Life,* 10 January 1949, pp. 86-90, 93-94, 96-98, 100-101. This article is reprinted in McCaffery, *Ernest Hemingway,* pp. 34-56; see below for full reference.

Hemingway, Gregory. *Papa: A Personal Memoir.* Boston: Houghton Mifflin, 1976; paper, Pocket Books, 1977.

Hemingway, Leicester. *My Brother, Ernest Hemingway.* [1962] New York: Fawcett World, 1972. Paper.

Hemingway, Mary. *How It Was.* New York: Knopf, 1976.

Hotchner, A. E. *Papa Hemingway: A Personal Memoir.* New York: Random House, 1966.

McLendon, James. *Papa: Hemingway in Key West, 1928-1940.* Miami: E. A. Seeman, n.d.; paper, Popular Library, 1974.

McCaffery, John K. M., ed. *Ernest Hemingway: The Man and His Work.* 1950. Reprint. New York: Cooper Square Publishers, 1969.

Miller, Madelaine Hemingway. *Ernie: Hemingway's Sister Sunny Remembers.* New York: Crown, 1975.

Montgomery, Constance Cappel. *Hemingway in Michigan.* New York: Fleet Publishing Corp., 1966.

Sanford, Marcelline Hemingway. *At the Hemingways: A Family Portrait.* Boston: Little, Brown and Company, 1962.

Audio-visual materials can be obtained from loan libraries, but at least two should be considered for purchase:

Ernest Hemingway Reading. [Record or cassette]. Caedmon, CDL 51185, 45 minutes, 10 seconds, with background notes by A. E. Hotchner and Mary Hemingway. The Nobel Prize address is especially useful. For information, write Caedmon Records, Inc., 505 Eighth Avenue, New York, New York 10018.

Ernest Hemingway. [Filmstrip]. The American Experience in Literature: Five Modern Novelists. Series No. 6911K. Encyclopaedia Britannica Educational Corporation, 1975, with cassette.

VALUABLE BOOKS: BIOGRAPHY AND CRITICISM

Baker, Carlos. *Hemingway: The Writer as Artist.* [1952] 4th rev. ed. Princeton, N.J.: Princeton University Press, 1972. Cloth and paper.

Baker, Sheridan. *Ernest Hemingway: An Introduction and Interpretation.* New York: Holt, Rinehart and Winston, 1967.

Bradbury, Ray. *I Sing the Body Electric.* New York: Alfred A. Knopf, 1969.

Cowley, Malcolm. *A Second Flowering: Works and Days of the Lost Generation.* New York: Viking, 1973; paper, Penguin, 1974.

DeFalco, Joseph. *The Hero in Hemingway's Short Stories.* 1963. Reprint. Darby, Pa.: Arden Library, 1977.

Falk, R. P., ed. *American Literature in Parody.* New York: Twayne, 1955.

Fenton, Charles A. *The Apprenticeship of Ernest Hemingway: The Early Years.* 1954. Reprint. New York: Octagon Books, 1975.

French, Warren C., and Kidd, Walter E., eds. *American Winners of the Nobel Literary Prize.* Norman: University of Oklahoma Press, 1968.

Frenz, Horst, ed., *Nobel Lectures: Literature, 1901–1967.* Amsterdam: Elsevier Publishing, 1969.

Hovey, Richard B. *Hemingway: The Inward Terrain.* Seattle: University of Washington Press, 1968.

Kiley, John. *Hemingway: An Old Friend Remembers.* New York: Hawthorn, 1965.

Klimo, Vernon (Jake), and Oursler, Will. *Hemingway and Jake.* [1972] New York: Popular Library, 1973. Paper.

Leggitt, John. *Ross and Tom: Two American Tragedies.* New York: Simon and Schuster, 1974.

Loeb, Harold. *The Way It Was.* New York: Criterion Books, 1959.

McCaffery, John K. M., ed. *Ernest Hemingway: The Man and His Work.* 1950. Reprint. New York: Cooper Square Publishers, n.d.

Ross, Lillian. *Portrait of Hemingway.* New York: Simon and Schuster, 1961. (Originally, *New Yorker,* May 13, 1950, Profile)

Rovit, Earl H. *Ernest Hemingway.* New York: Twayne, 1963; paper, College and University Press, 1963.

Sarason, Bertram D. *Hemingway and the Sun Set.* Washington, D.C.: National Cash Register Company/Microcard Editions, 1972.

Stephens, Robert O., ed. *Ernest Hemingway: The Critical Reception.* New York: Burt Franklin, 1977.

Stuckey, W. J. *The Pulitzer Prize Novels.* Norman: University of Oklahoma Press, 1966.

Waldhorn, Arthur. *A Reader's Guide to Ernest Hemingway.* New York: Farrar, Straus, and Giroux, 1972. Cloth and paper.

Watts, Emily S. *Ernest Hemingway and the Arts.* Urbana: University of Illinois Press, 1971.

Weeks, Robert P., ed. *Hemingway: A Collection of Critical Essays.* Englewood Cliffs, N.J.: Prentice-Hall, 1962.

Young, Philip. *Ernest Hemingway: A Reconsideration.* 2nd ed. University Park: Pennsylvania State University Press, 1966.

ARTICLES AND ESSAYS: BIOGRAPHY AND CRITICISM

Baker, Carlos. "The Boy and the Lions." In *20th Century Interpretations of "The Old Man and the Sea,"* edited by Katherine T. Jobes, pp. 27–33. Englewood Cliffs, N.J.: Prentice-Hall, 1968.

Burgum, Edwin Berry. "Ernest Hemingway and the Psychology of the Lost Generation." In his *The Novel and the World's Dilemma,* pp. 184–204. New York: Oxford University Press, 1947.

Cowley, Malcolm. "Hemingway and the Hero." *New Republic,* 4 December 1944, pp. 754–58.

Eastman, Max. "Bull in the Afternoon." *New Republic,* 7 June 1933, pp. 94–97.

Fiedler, Leslie. *Love and Death in the American Novel,* pp. 304–9, 350–52. New York: Criterion, 1960.

Fuchs, Daniel. "Ernest Hemingway, Literary Critic." *American Literature* 36 (1965):431–51.

Kazin, Alfred. *On Native Grounds.* New York: Harcourt, Brace, 1942; paper, 1972, pp. 393–99.

Lewis, Wyndam. "The Dumb Ox: A Study of Ernest Hemingway." *The American Review* 3 (1934):289–312.

Plimpton, George. "The Art of Fiction, XXI: Hemingway." *Paris Review,* no. 18 (1958), pp. 61–89. Also in *Writers at Work: The Paris Interviews,* Second series, pp. 215–39. New York: Viking, 1963.

Van Gelder, Robert. "Ernest Hemingway Talks of Work and War." In *Writers and Writing,* pp. 95–98. New York: Scribner's, 1946.

Warren, Robert Penn. "Ernest Hemingway." *Kenyon Review* 9 (1947):52–60. Also in *Literary Opinion in America,* edited by Morton D. Zabel, vol. 2, pp. 444–63. 1951. Reprint. Magnolia, Massachusetts: Peter Smith, 1968.

Wilson, Edmund. "Hemingway: Bourbon Gauge of Morale." In his *The Wound and the Bow: Seven Studies in Literature,* pp. 214–42. New York: Oxford University Press, 1947.

Young, Philip. "Loser Take Nothing." In *20th Century Interpretations of "A Farewell to Arms,"* edited by Jay Gellens, pp. 28–32. Englewood Cliffs, N.J.: Prentice-Hall, 1970.

Young, Philip. "Our Hemingway Man." *Kenyon Review* 26 (1964):676–707.

BOOKS: CHECKLIST OF PRIMARY SOURCES

Three Stories and Ten Poems. [1923] Bloomfield Hills, Mich.: Bruccoli Clark Books, 1977.

In Our Time. [1924, 1925] New York: Scribner's, 1930. Cloth and paper.

The Torrents of Spring. [1926] New York: Scribner's, 1972. Cloth and paper.

The Sun Also Rises. New York: Scribner's, 1926. Cloth and paper.

Men Without Women. New York: Scribner's, 1927. Paper.

A Farewell to Arms. New York: Scribner's, 1929. Cloth and paper.

Death in the Afternoon. New York: Scribner's, 1932. Cloth and paper.

Winner Take Nothing. New York: Scribner's, 1933. Paper.

Green Hills of Africa. New York: Scribner's, 1935. Cloth and paper.

To Have and Have Not. New York: Scribner's, 1937. Cloth and paper.

The Fifth Column and the First Forty-Nine Stories. New York: Scribner's, 1938.

For Whom the Bell Tolls. New York: Scribner's, 1940. Cloth and paper.

Across the River and into the Trees. New York: Scribner's, 1950. Cloth and paper.

The Old Man and the Sea. [1952] New York: Scribner's, 1961. Cloth and paper.

Posthumous Publications

The Wild Years, edited by Gene Z. Hanrahan. New York: Dell, 1962. Seventy-three articles from the Toronto *Star*.

A Moveable Feast. New York: Scribner's, 1964. Cloth and paper.

By-Line: Ernest Hemingway, Selected Articles and Dispatches of Four Decades, edited by William White. New York: Scribner's, 1967. Cloth and paper.

The Fifth Column and Four Stories of the Spanish Civil War. New York: Scribner's, 1969. Cloth and paper.

Islands in the Stream. New York: Scribner's, 1970. Cloth and paper.

Ernest Hemingway, Cub Reporter: Kansas City Star Stories, edited by M. Bruccoli. Pittsburgh: University of Pittsburgh Press, 1970.

Ernest Hemingway's Apprenticeship, Oak Park, 1916–1917, edited by M. Bruccoli. Washington, D.C.: Microcard Editions, 1971. Uncollected early writings, Oak Park, Illinois, High School *Tabula* and *Trapeze*.

EDUCATIONAL FILMS

Hemingway. NBC: McGraw-Hill. 54 min., b/w.

Hemingway's Spain: "Death in the Afternoon." ABC: McGraw-Hill, 1969. 15 min., color.

Hemingway's Spain: "For Whom the Bell Tolls." ABC: McGraw-Hill, 1969. 19 min., color.

Hemingway's Spain: "The Sun Also Rises." ABC: McGraw-Hill, 1969. 17 min., color.

Hemingway's Spain: The Sun Also Rises. ABC: McGraw-Hill, 1969. 17 min., color.

My Old Man. Encyclopaedia Britannica Educational Corp. 27 min., color.

Soldier's Home. Learning in Focus, Inc.-Coronet Instructional Films, 1977. 41 min., color.

FILMSTRIP-RECORD/CASSETTES

Ernest Hemingway [Filmstrip]. Listening Library, NOOCFX, and cassette. Covers his life from World War I to his suicide. For information, write Listening Library, Inc., 1 Park Avenue, Old Greenwich, Connecticut 06870.

Ernest Hemingway [Filmstrip]. 2 rolls. Educational Dimensions Corp., no. 708, and 2 12-min. discs or 2 cassettes, 15 min. each. For information, write Educational Dimensions Corp., Box 488, Great Neck, New York 11022.

Ernest Hemingway: The Man—A Biographical Interpretation with Carlos Baker [Filmstrip]. 2 rolls. Guidance Associates, 7F–508 307 (LPs) or 7F–508 299 (cassettes), and 2 12-in. discs or 2 cassettes, 16 or 17 min. For information, write Guidance Associates, Pleasantville, New York 10570.

RECORDS AND CASSETTES

Grebstein, Sheldon. *For Whom the Bell Tolls*. Listening Library, N96CX, cassette. Lecture.

Hemingway. Listening Library, N98R, 2 12-in. discs. Memories of the writer from his friends, about his public and private life.

Hemingway, Ernest. *The Old Man and the Sea*. Charlton Heston, reader. Caedmon, TC 2084, 2 12-in. discs or 2 cassettes.

Hotchner, A. E. *Hotchner on Hemingway*. Listening Library, N100CX, cassette.

Hotling, Charles K. *Ernest Hemingway: "The Old Man and the Sea."* Listening Library, N94CX, cassette.

Wylder, Delbert. *The Early Short Stories of Ernest Hemingway*. Listening Library, N101CX, cassette.

——. *The Middle Short Stories of Ernest Hemingway*. Listening Library, N102CX, cassette.

——. *The Late Short Stories of Ernest Hemingway*. Listening Library, N103CX, cassette.

Young, Philip. *A Farewell to Arms*. Listening Library, N97CX, cassette.

——. *The Sun Also Rises*. Listening Library, N95CX, cassette.

For information on the above listings, write Listening Library, Inc., 1 Park Avenue, Old Greenwich, Connecticut 06870.

PICTURES AND POSTERS

Ernest Hemingway [Poster]. Eight Masters of Modern Fiction series. Includes Fitzgerald, Hemingway, Wolfe, Baldwin, Salinger, McCullers, Faulkner, and Steinbeck. Scholastic Book Services, set of 8 pictures, 15 x 20 in. For information, write Scholastic Book Services, 50 West 44th Street, New York, New York 10036.

Ernest Hemingway [Picture]. Perfection Form Co., KJ95948, color, 8 1/2 x 11 in.

A Farewell to Arms [Pictures]. Hemingway series. Perfection Form Co., KJ3012, set of 5 pictures, 10 x 13 in.

For Whom the Bell Tolls [Pictures]. Hemingway series. Perfection Form Co., KJ3072, set of 2 pictures, 8 1/2 x 11 in.

The Old Man and the Sea [Pictures]. Hemingway series. Perfection Form Co., KJ6132, set of 10 pictures.

The Sun Also Rises [Pictures]. Hemingway series. Perfection Form Co., KJ7692, set of 10 pictures, 10 x 13 in.

For information on the above listings, with the exception of the first, write Perfection Form Company, 1000 North Second Avenue, Logan, Iowa 51546.

Note: the instructor should try to secure a copy of *Life,* July 14, 1961, pp. 51–72, for a cover story-photo essay on Hemingway.

HOLLYWOOD FILMS

Most of the Hollywood films based on Hemingway writings are still available through loan libraries. Check with your A-V director for catalogs and prices.

Adventures of a Young Man. Based on the book *In Our Time.* 1962, Twentieth Century-Fox. The script was prepared from a TV series adaptation of ten Nick Adams stories done by A. E. Hotchner. Parts of *A Farewell to Arms* were added to the film. Producer: Jerry Wald. Richard Beymer (Nick); Jessica Tandy (Mrs. Adams); Arthur Kennedy (Dr. Adams); Paul Newman ("The Battler"). Director: Martin Ritt. Color, 145 minutes.

A Farewell to Arms. 1932, Paramount. Gary Cooper (Frederic); Helen Hayes (Catherine); Adolphe Menjou (Rinaldi). Director: Henry King. B/W, 78 minutes. Also, 1957, Twentieth Century-Fox. Rock Hudson (Frederic); Jennifer Jones (Catherine); Vittorio de Sica (Rinaldi). Director: Charles Vidor. Color, 151 minutes.

For Whom the Bell Tolls. 1943, Paramount. Gary Cooper (Jordan); Ingrid Bergman (Maria); Katina Paxinou (Pilar); Akim Tamiroff (Pablo). Director: Sam Wood. Color, 156 minutes.

Islands in the Stream. 1977, Paramount. George C. Scott (Thomas Hudson) with David Hemmings (Eddy), Clare Bloom (Audrey). Director: Franklin J. Schaffner. Color, 110 minutes.

The Killers. 1946, Universal. Burt Lancaster (Ole Anderson). Director: Robert Siedmak. B/W, 102 minutes. Also, 1964, Universal. Lee Marvin (Charlie), Angie Dickinson (Sheila Farr), Ronald Reagan (Browning), John Cassavetes (Johnny North). Director: Don Siegel. Color, 95 minutes.

The Macomber Affair. 1947, United Artists. Gregory Peck (Macomber); Joan Bennett (Margot); Robert Preston (Wilson). Director: Z. Korda. B/W, 89 minutes.

The Old Man and the Sea. 1958, Warner Brothers. Spencer Tracy (Santiago). Director: John Sturges. Color, 86 minutes.

The Sun Also Rises. 1957, Twentieth Century-Fox. Tyrone Power (Jake); Ava Gardner (Brett); Mel Ferrer (Robert Cohn); Errol Flynn (Mike Campbell); Eddie Albert (Bill Gorton). Director: Henry King. Color, 129 minutes.

The Snows of Kilimanjaro. 1952, Twentieth Century-Fox. Gregory Peck (Harry) with Susan Hayward (Helen) and Ava Gardner (Cynthia). Director: Henry King. Color, 117 minutes.

To Have and Have Not. 1944, Warner Brothers. Humphrey Bogart (Harry); Lauren Bacall (Mrs. Morgan). Director: Howard Hawks. B/W, 100 minutes.

Under My Skin. Based on the short story "My Old Man." 1950, Twentieth Century-Fox. John Garfield (Dan Butler) and Luther Adler (Louis Bark). Director: Jean Negulesco. B/W, 68 minutes.

AUTHOR

Brooke Workman is Instructor of English and Humanities and a supervisor of student teachers at West High School, Iowa City, Iowa. He has had over twenty years of experience in the teaching of English at the junior high and high school levels. His publications include numerous journal articles and book reviews and *Teaching the Decades: A Humanities Approach to American Civilization* (NCTE, 1975). Workman holds a Ph.D. in American Civilization from the University of Iowa.

61716